Twayne's United States Authors Series

Sylvia E. Bowman, *Editor*

INDIANA UNIVERSITY

George W. Cable

GEORGE W. CABLE

by **PHILIP BUTCHER**

Morgan State College

Twayne Publishers, Inc. :: New York

TO MY MOTHER

Preface

MODERN critics, often unfamiliar with the body of his works and only superficially acquainted with his major books, have tended to praise George W. Cable for his faults and to damn him for his virtues. The best criticism of his work is marred by serious factual errors. On the other hand, some of the most accurate treatments of his life and times seem grossly mistaken in their interpretations and critical judgments, both of his works and his character. Some scholars, bemused by the image Cable built of himself, have placed him on a different pedestal from the one he deserves. Others have denounced the man and attempted to dismiss his work as unimportant by placing it in a narrow pigeonhole marked "Local Color." Although he has been the subject of a number of recent scholarly studies, and several of his books have appeared in paperback reprints, Cable is little known to the general reading public. His early writing is studied in college survey courses in American literature and one or another of his stories finds its way into textbooks and anthologies; but his name is confused with that of James Branch Cabell and his achievement equated with that of Grace King or Kate Chopin. Few people realize that he published two novels, the last of a career that stretched back over forty-five years, in 1918.

This book is designed as a critical study of Cable's works set against the background of his life and times. It attempts to present the essential biographical facts in such a way as to give depth to a portrait too often drawn, in reverence or pardonable ignorance, only in outline. It endeavors to relate that portrait to Cable's major works, which are discussed in the general order of their initial book publication. *George W. Cable* undertakes no detailed treatment of his articles on Bible study, gardening, etc., as these are of no great consequence to his achievement as a literary artist, or of the essays on the race question. The latter have been appraised in a number of able studies, are readily accessible, and are of such quality and moment as to demand that the interested student read them for himself.

The supposition that each of Cable's books is a product of his experiences, circumstances, and character is basic to this volume. Footnotes have been kept to a minimum, but it should be clear that I have relied heavily on the many articles and books that treat Cable's life, though my interpretation of the significance of particular facts is occasionally at variance with that of my source. Considerable information presented here is the product of very recent research, assisted by a grant from the Faculty Research Committee of Morgan State College; it is derived from interviews, manuscripts, and miscellaneous printed materials not previously available for study. For cooperation and assistance I am indebted to many people it is not feasible to name. Among those who must be mentioned are Miss Anna Gertrude Brewster and her sisters; Mrs. Thomas Shepherd and Miss Mary Persis Crafts, who brought to my attention documents in the archives of the Northampton Historical Society; Mrs. Alma S. Edwards, executive secretary of The People's Institute, who has given invaluable aid for several years; Miss Esther M. Wyman, whose work in the Smith College archives turned up many items of interest; and Mr. Carl Walz, who helped me to acquire various reference and manuscript materials. While he was president of The People's Institute, Mr. William H. Brownell did much to facilitate my research. So did other citizens of Northampton, former residents, and Smith College alumnae who knew G. W. Cable.

To Mr. Lawrence E. Wikander, Librarian of Forbes Library, I am also indebted for extensive cooperation and for much of my information about the Northampton Social and Literary Club. Mrs. Caroline Lord, of Francestown, N. H., generously granted access to the extant journals of Clarence B. Roote, the property of the George Holmes Bixby Memorial Library. I must thank also the librarians and curators of special collections at Butler Library, Columbia University; Howard-Tilton Memorial Library, Tulane University; and the Schomburg Collection, New York Public Library. Mrs. Dorothy B. Porter and Dr. W. Montague Cobb of Howard University made special materials available to me. The letters of Mr. Harry B. Taplin and the late Miss Adelene Moffat which are quoted or published in this book are printed with their permission, for which I am grateful. Quotations from those of Cable's books which are still in copyright appear here with permission of Charles Scribner's Sons. To Mr. William E.

Preface

Weir, I am obliged less for his careful perusal of many pages of old correspondence than for a long friendship I appreciate more than I can suitably acknowledge. Finally, the forbearance of my daughters, Wendy and Laurel, and the editorial assistance of my wife, Ruth, have been of incalculable value in helping me to complete this study. Its shortcomings may not be attributed to inadequate aid or encouragement, and it goes without saying that accountability for factual errors and mistakes of judgment, which Professor Sylvia E. Bowman has exerted her talents and energies to eliminate, must be mine alone.

Morgan State College
Baltimore, Md.

PHILIP BUTCHER

Contents

Chronology

1844   George Washington Cable born in New Orleans, October 12.

1859   On the death of his father, Cable left high school and went to work.

1863   Enlisted in Confederate Army, October 9.

1869   Married Louise Stewart Bartlett on December 7. Began to contribute to New Orleans *Picayune*.

1870   First child, Louise, born on November 26. Three other daughters and one son born by 1877.

1871   Attempts to arrange book publication of his fugitive *Picayune* pieces were unsuccessful.

1872   At work on his short stories.

1873   Cable met his "discoverer," Edward King. " 'Sieur George" published. Other stories followed in next three years.

1875   Cable met his publishers on a trip to the North.

1877   H. H. Boyesen initiated a correspondence of crucial importance to Cable's literary career.

1878   George Boardman Cable, the author's four-year-old son, died in the yellow fever epidemic.

1879   Collected stories, *Old Creole Days*, published. First installments of *The Grandissimes*.

1880   George E. Waring gave Cable commission to report on New Orleans for the *Tenth Census*. Second visit to New York.

1881   Census report and *Madame Delphine* published. Family spent the summer in New Hampshire. Cable abandoned his clerical employment to make belles-lettres his occupation.

1883   Lectures at Johns Hopkins and first public readings from his works. Daughter Isabel born. Cable overcame his scruples against theater going. First installments of *Dr. Sevier.*

1884 "The Convict Lease System in the Southern States" and *The Creoles of Louisiana* published. Southerners joined Creoles in resenting Cable's work. First visit to Northampton, Mass. Family settled in Connecticut. Joint readings with Mark Twain.

1885 With publication of "The Freedman's Case in Equity," Cable became notorious as champion of Negro rights. Son William born. Family moved to Northampton. *The Silent South.*

1886 Beginning of the Home Culture Clubs.

1887 Cable and Adelene Moffat met in Tennessee. Bible classes in Northampton and Boston.

1888 Open Letter Club organized. "The Negro Question" and *Bonaventure.*

1889 Adelene Moffat in Northampton as general secretary of the Home Culture Clubs. Daughter Dorothea born. *Strange True Stories of Louisiana.*

1890 Open Letter Club abandoned. *The Negro Question.* Cable's mother died.

1891 Cable's writings on Bible study and teaching ended with publication of *The Busy Man's Bible.*

1892 First issue of Home Culture Clubs house organ, the *Letter.* The Cables moved into "Tarryawhile." Last essay on Southern problems and *A Memory of Roswell Smith* published.

1894 *John March, Southerner* published in *Scribner's Magazine.* Richard Thorndyke Smith emerges as Cable's alter ego.

1896 James M. Barrie visited "Tarryawhile." The *Letter* became the *Symposium,* which expired after three issues.

1897 Cable returned to Northampton after a short term in New York as editor of *Current Literature.*

1898 Cable made a triumphal tour of England, reading from his works. Visit with Andrew Carnegie in Scotland.

1899 *Strong Hearts.*

1901 *The Cavalier.*

1902 *Bylow Hill.* About a dozen years after Cable's first efforts
to prepare his works for the stage, a dramatization of
The Cavalier played on Broadway.

1903 Andrew Carnegie gave $50,000 for a Home Culture club-
house. Cable saw himself as founder of a people's college.

1904 Cable's wife died in February.

1905 After the dedication of "Carnegie House," Cable and his
daughter Lucy took a vacation in England.

1906 Married Eva C. Stevenson, November 24.

1907 Adelene Moffat fired. Rumors circulated in Northampton.
Home Culture Clubs under public scrutiny.

1908 William Cable, son, died. *Kincaid's Battery.*

1909 Home Culture Clubs renamed The People's Institute.
"Posson Jone'" and *Père Raphaël.*

1914 *Gideon's Band* and *The Amateur Garden.*

1918 *The Flower of the Chapdelaines* and *Lovers of Louisiana.*

1923 Mrs. Eva Cable died in June; Cable married Hanna
Cowing in December.

1925 Cable died, on January 31, in St. Petersburg, Fla.

George W. Cable

CHAPTER 1

"Parson in a Crap Game"

T HE NAME of George W. Cable naturally calls to mind, as a kind of conditioned reflex, the name of his native city, New Orleans, which, together with its environs, served as his principal subject from 1873, when his first Creole[1] story appeared, to 1918, when his last two novels were published. Other noted authors have lived in the fabulous city and written about it, but it was largely Cable, in many respects "as much a misfit in New Orleans as a parson in a crap game,"[2] who gave its exotic history, quaint customs, and conflicting cultures permanent fame in American literature.

Only three American cities—New York, Philadelphia, and Baltimore—could boast of more residents than the 130,000 people who lived in New Orleans when Cable was born there on October 12, 1844. It had not been an American city very long, and it had not lost its distinctly international quality. Although Louisiana had become American territory in 1803 and a State in 1812, New Orleans was still strikingly different from the other cities of the nation. Founded in 1718, it had been made the capital of the French colony in 1722 and was dominated by French culture even when it was a Spanish possession from 1763 to 1801. By the 1840's the Creoles, descendants of the French and Spanish settlers, were declining in influence; much of their wealth and power had passed into the hands of the more enterprising Americans.

The Americans were of varied types, ranging from the crude Kentucky and Tennessee boatmen on the bustling Mississippi to the more refined descendants of the English and Americans who had entered Louisiana in the eighteenth century. In addition to the people of French, Spanish, and English stock, there were some Acadians, whose ancestors had been exiled from Nova Scotia in 1755, and some citizens who could trace their ancestry to the Indians. Over the years, but particularly in the first decade of the nineteenth century, thousands of assorted refugees arrived from the West Indies, fleeing the slave uprisings or the effects of the Napoleonic wars. Differences in custom, language, religion —differences emblematic of status in caste-ridden New Orleans— tended to be preserved and emphasized. It was a city of contrasts, a city of conflicts.

When Cable began to write he was astute enough to see its contrasts and the colorful history behind them as a mine of literary source material—in an age which prized exactly the kind of ore he had come upon—and its conflicts as symbols of the perplexing issues plaguing the nation after the Civil War. In large measure those issues, like the "irrepressible conflict" itself, could be traced to slavery, which had come to Louisiana from the Caribbean. There it flourished in the sixteenth century, based on the demand for cheap labor to produce tobacco, indigo, cotton, rice, sugar, and rum. The first settlements in Louisiana were established in 1699, and by 1712, before New Orleans was founded, twenty African slaves were in the colony. Even in the early years, all the Negroes in Louisiana were not slaves. When Governor Bienville led a force against the Choctaw Indians in 1735, his command included, in addition to 545 white soldiers, forty-five Negroes whose officers were free blacks. Earlier, in 1724, Bienville's Black Code acknowledged the presence of free Negroes by making provision for the disposition of their children.

The *gens de couleur libres* became numerous as the years passed; and, by the time of Cable's birth, they constituted a considerable portion of the population.[3] Among them were mulattoes, quadroons, and octoroons; and some bore in their veins a fraction of African blood so minute as to be imperceptible. The freedom of the "f.m.c." and "f.w.c." (free men and women of color) was a relative one, for while their legal, economic, and social status was above that of the slaves it was far inferior to that of the whites. Yet they were an element of some conse-quence in the community. They fought with distinction under Andrew Jackson in the Battle of New Orleans in 1815; but, like the Creoles, they gave cultural allegiance to France.

Free men of color published, in 1843, *L'Album Litteraire*, a journal which offered fiction, essays, and poetry. French critics gave special praise to three of the contributors, including Victor Sejour, who had twenty-one plays produced on the Paris stage, three of them running at different theaters at the same time. Some of the poems were reprinted in 1845 in *Les Cenelles*, a volume that might be called the first anthology of poetry by American Negroes, though the verse is in French and the authors, who used Lamartine and Berenger as models, would not have described themselves as Negroes or Americans.[4] In 1840, a year or two before the beginning of public education for whites in New Orleans, the Ecole des Orphelins Indigents was founded. Among the free colored people who supported this free school for colored children were Mme. Couvent, who left a trust fund for its establishment; Aristide Mary, who left it $5,000; and Thomy Lafon. Worth half a million dollars when he died, Lafon was so highly regarded as a public benefactor that the state legislature ordered a bust placed on display in a public institution.

The opening of libraries, the revival of the historical society, and the quick spread of public education which took place in the 1840's enriched the city but left it lagging well behind other American cities in these and other civic developments. A particular problem which affected New Orleans throughout its history remained unsolved, almost unattacked: the plagues and epidemics which raged nearly every year. The port and river traffic (thousands of steamboats and flatboats docked annually), open street gutters, floods, the semitropical climate, inattention to the rules of sanitation, and the practice of burying the dead in tombs above ground encouraged small pox, yellow fever, and cholera to take a heavy toll of lives in recurring visits. Between 1810 and 1837 there were fifteen epidemics of yellow fever. In 1835 cholera killed one in every ten of the 150,000 inhabitants.

But the threat of pestilence did little to deter the immigrants of all kinds who flocked in, lured by the promise of excitement, prosperity, or a haven from some less tolerant homeland. Refugees from Cuba, West Indian Creoles, came in droves between 1804 and 1810, when the population doubled. It doubled again in the 1840's, when Irish and Germans, largely unskilled laborers, entered at a rate of 30,000 a year and almost threatened to crowd the slaves out of service. As old and as cosmopolitan as the Crescent City was, and as static as was its Creole society, it

[21]

had many of the attractions of the frontier, where the daring and industrious and fortunate might win a quick prosperity. It was, especially for the intruding Americans so scorned by the Creoles, a city of opportunity.

So Cable's parents, neither of whom was a native of Louisiana, thought it to be. The father, George Washington Cable, was born in Virginia, where his ancestors had settled before the Revolution, but he was reared in Pennsylvania and Indiana.[5] Rebecca Boardman Cable, the mother, was born in Indiana of New England stock. After their marriage in 1834, Cable was successively a cooper, a tavern proprietor, and a businessman. After he was ruined in the Great Panic of 1837, the family traveled fifteen hundred miles down the Ohio and Mississippi and settled in New Orleans. Seven years later when the fifth child, George Washington Cable, was born in a house on Annunciation Square, the family had attained a measure of prosperity. The father's business interests were varied; for a while he was a partner in an enterprise supplying groceries to river boats; at one time he owned a part interest in a Mississippi steamer captained by a cousin who left for the California gold fields in 1849. As the lean and the fat years alternated, the family moved to different homes several times. There were separations, too, the wife and children returning to Indiana to stay with the Boardmans while the father sought work or improved business conditions in New Orleans. After such a separation the family reassembled in 1854, but the financial difficulties were not over. Broken in spirit and health by his failures, the father died in 1859. Young George was fourteen, the oldest boy in the family. He left high school and took his father's job in the customhouse to help support the family. For the rest of his life, G. W. Cable was never really free of financial problems.

With the outbreak of the Civil War in 1861, Cable's job at the customhouse ended, and he became cashier for a firm of wholesale grocers. New Orleans fell before the assault of Union ships in April, 1862, and the city was soon occupied by Northern troops. The Cables refused to take the oath of allegiance required by General Benjamin F. Butler's orders and declared themselves enemies of the United States. Cable, in short pants, and his two sisters were banished from the city. This gave the slight youngster his chance to enlist in the Confederate cavalry. Only five feet five inches tall, he weighed about a hundred pounds (at his heaviest in later years he weighed barely ten pounds more); but he proved to be an able fighting man. Twice wounded, he shifted to the artillery near the close of the war.

Certainly he was an unusual soldier, for he found time to study, to practice drawing, and to read the Bible and other books. As a clerk in a unit under General Nathan Bedford Forrest's command, Cable wrote manumission papers when Forrest freed his slaves. The war service was a time of maturing and learning for the studious youth, who used every opportunity to educate himself generally and who gave thought to the issues that had brought on the struggle in which he was engaged. At the war's close he had come to question the right of secession and, perhaps, the justice and practical wisdom of slavery as an institution.

On his return to civilian life, young Cable worked at a succession of small jobs—errand boy, grocery clerk, accountant. He seems to have been normally appreciative of the charms of pretty girls and to have had a number of mild love affairs before his marriage, on December 7, 1869, to Louise Stewart Bartlett, a beautiful young New Orleans neighbor of Northern extraction.

I *Journalist*

Beginning in February, 1870, Cable wrote for the New Orleans *Picayune* a column which appeared ninety times during the following eighteen months. The subject matter of the personal essays, signed "Drop Shot," was varied. Toward the end of the series the columns came to stress literary matters, including appraisals of the novels Cable had read. Many of the columns, however, were devoted to civic problems and showed the young author's alertness to public affairs, his didactic inclinations, and his willingness to reach judgments independent of or contrary to the views of the majority of his fellows. Some of the offerings were poetry, which Cable came to recognize was not his forte though, like his father, he wrote verses all his life. An analysis of the "Drop Shot" series shows that it reveals or foreshadows all the qualities Cable demonstrated more impressively in later years.

As early as 1871, Cable served the *Picayune* as reporter as well as columnist. In reporting a meeting of public school teachers, he took offense at the compulsory intermingling of white and Negro teachers and expressed in print his resentment at this violation of segregation. Other papers took up the clamor; but, to the disappointment of his employers, Cable let the matter drop. When he wrote again on segregation in the schools in letters to the New Orleans *Bulletin* in 1875, it was to attack segregation—not its violation.

Evidently feeling that journalism in either form he had experienced was neither a congenial nor a sufficiently rewarding occupation, Cable stopped reporting when his column ended. He was ambitious now for a different kind of literary achievement. Hoping for book publication, he prepared a manuscript, compiled from his column, which he described as presenting scenes and characters representative of the peculiar social order of New Orleans. Scribner's, the only publisher willing to examine the work, turned it down, though Cable offered to pay the full cost of an edition of two thousand copies. The rejection merely strengthened his determination to get a book in print some day.

It turned out that he was not through with journalism. In February, 1872, he wrote a series of articles on New Orleans churches and charities, research for which carried him to the records of the colorful history of Louisiana. The material was so fascinating and provocative that Cable began to collect and document the romantic stories of his region's past; as early as 1872, he had begun work on his own Creole stories. He wrote some newspaper book reviews and a series of articles designed to expose the powerful Louisiana Lottery Company. In this reform movement Cable was only the anonymous author of the propaganda. The movement failed. Later when he entered the lists against civic lassitude and corruption, it was as organizer and public servant as well as journalist.

II *Early Stories*

Cable was not the first to see the history of exotic Louisiana as a source for literature. Had he happened to begin his career at a less propitious moment, his talents might never have been accorded their desserts. After the Civil War the course of

American writing was directed to a considerable extent by the policies of the major periodicals, which, as agents of national policy, were anxious to reduce sectional animosities.[6] Though they set standards in literary taste, they had to consider a reading public which, because of the war, was interested in people and places scattered from coast to coast and border to border. Local color writing, with its stress on the oddities of speech and manners in the differing regions of the reunited nation, was not exclusively a literary phenomenon. Certainly it was in accord with the program of *Scribner's Monthly.*

Edward King, who visited New Orleans early in 1873 in connection with the Great South papers he was preparing for this journal, was in search of just such material as Cable was accumulating in his desk. Quick to appreciate the merit of the stories Cable read to him shortly before his departure, King brought them to the attention of his firm and urged their acceptance. One story, "Bibi," had too much horror and violence for editors determined that nothing should appear in their magazine that might offend the most sensitive young readers. Another, "'Sieur George," was accepted after Cable revised it and was published in *Scribner's Monthly* for October, 1873.

Slowly over the next few years came other stories of Creole Louisiana. *Scribner's Monthly* printed "Belles Demoiselles Plantation" in April and "'Tite Poulette" in October, 1874; "Jean-ah Poquelin" and 'Madame Délicieuse" appeared in May and August, 1875; and "Café des Exilés" was in the issue for March, 1876. "Posson Jone'," rejected by several editors because of the demeaning role of the parson, finally appeared in *Appleton's Journal*, April 1, 1876. "Don Joaquin," published in *Harper's Magazine* in January, 1876, Cable evidently wished to disown later.

Although none of the publishers Cable approached about issuing the collected stories as a book was willing to undertake the venture, the appearance of his Creole stories in the magazines had brought him some favorable national attention and had made him, for a short time, a minor local celebrity; but they were important more as the promise of future achievement than as distinction already attained. Moreover, pay for the tales averaged only about seventy dollars each, too little to justify the time Cable spent on them. After November, 1875, he ignored his publisher's invitation to submit more stories. Financial burdens kept him at his accounting desk and pressed him to find additional employment to support his growing family.

On September 2, 1875, Cable wrote to his children: "When I hear that you are enjoying the pleasures of the seaside, I am so delighted that I open my sleeve slyly and laugh right into it till it is as full of laugh as a bathhouse. I have a hole in the elbow for this very purpose. A man named *Pauvreté* (Poverty), a Frenchman, made it for me for nothing."[7] When Lucy Cable was born two months later, the family included two other daughters, Louise and Mary, and a son, George Boardman Cable. Another daughter, Margaret, was born in 1877, when the Cables were in a house of their own for the first time. Before this the family had moved from one rented house to another, each of them with a room for Cable's mother but none with enough space for a study. In 1876 Cable bought (or began to buy) two lots on Eighth Street in the "Garden District," the American section of New Orleans opposite the Creole district. The Cable home, 1313 Eighth Street, was a cottage that had been built in 1874. Painted in soft shades of red and olive, it was surrounded by a garden, and there was a veranda resting on square brick columns. Busy with the three jobs he needed in order to pay for the house and meet his other obligations, Cable had no time for writing.

III *Old Creole Days Published*

Yet *Old Creole Days*, his collected stories, appeared in 1879. The circumstances pertaining to the publication of Cable's first book deserve examination in some detail; for, properly interpreted, they provide an insight into the personality of a complex man who, altogether too often, has been accepted in accordance with his representation of himself. The man responsible for getting the book into print was Hjalmar H. Boyesen.

Though younger than Cable and an American only since his arrival in New York from Norway in 1869, Boyesen was a consequential literary figure as a successful author of poems, criticism, stories, and novels by the time he initiated a correspondence with Cable on February 18, 1877.[8] He did so because he was impressed by the excellence of the Creole tales that had appeared in *Scribner's Monthly*; and, having seen nothing in print by Cable in recent months, he was anxious to encourage the Southern author to continue or resume his literary career. Boyesen, whose tremendous energy let him hold a professorship at Cornell and yet produce for the best American magazines at a prolific rate, was acquainted with the most influential editors. He wanted to place himself at Cable's service. Already he had done much by praising the Creole stories to his students and friends, among them Richard Watson Gilder, the *Scribner's* editor who sat in judgment on Cable's manuscripts.

Boyesen wrote to Cable in 1879 of his admiration for his writing and of his own pleasure in learning from Gilder that Cable was busy with a novel. Although Cable's reply is not extant—as is the case with some of his later letters to his new friend—he evidently sent to Boyesen, whom he must have known by reputation and hence would have wished to please, a brief sketch of the plot of a novel. (Years later, in his "After-Thoughts of a Story-Teller," published in the *North American Review* for January, 1894, Cable said that, as far as he could remember, his first novel was written without any preliminary plan.) Boyesen read the sketch, he wrote on March 17, "with a glow of delight"; he praised the characters Cable described, though their role in the projected work was not detailed. The prospectus, however slight, was enough to raise Boyesen's enthusiasm.

Cable made no reply until April 27, when he wrote to say his health had prevented him from doing any further work on the project. Doggedly Boyesen pressed the matter in a letter in November, urging Cable to proceed with the book. He lamented the unstimulating nature of the South—a "literary Sahara"—and assured Cable he could count on "hearty friends and warm admirers" in the North. Cable replied in a long, characteristic, and illuminating letter on January 3, 1878. He confessed that he had done nothing on his novel since sending the brief sketch the previous March. The debilitating weather and the threat of inflammation of the lungs had driven him to take a month's vacation in the fall. Now he was fully occupied with his jobs: bookkeeper and cashier in a cotton house; clerk of the Cotton Exchange, and treasurer's clerk of the National Cotton Exchange. Efforts to resign one or another of these jobs to use the time for writing only led his employers to double his salary, according to Cable. He said it would be feasible for him to write for the magazines only if editors would pay twice what they did. Yet literary ambitions drove him and he was determined to get back to writing when he finished paying for his "pretty little house—a couple of years or so." (This inaccuracy is not unique in Cable's correspondence. When he sold the house in 1885—seven years later—for $5,500, he owed a mortgage of $4,000 on the property.) He agreed wholeheartedly with Boyesen's strictures on the South and closed his letter with the sort of ingratiating sentiments often to be found in his later correspondence with people whose esteem he valued: "I yearn toward the North. To me *that* is the South. There is the sunlight & flowers and fruits—there is Boyesen."

Not content with encouraging his friend to resume writing or with telling publishers of the promise of his work, Boyesen took drastic action to assist Cable's prospects. He went to Blair Scribner and, by guaranteeing the firm against financial loss, prevailed on the publisher to reverse his earlier rejection of Cable's plan for book publication of the Creole stories. Boyesen's generous act rescued the delicate tales from oblivion and ultimately saved Cable from a lifetime of the clerical pursuits which he told Boyesen he found so distasteful. In addition to sponsoring Cable's first book, Boyesen was also spiritual godfather to his second. He somehow conveyed to the publishers his enthusiasm for the prospectus of Cable's first novel. Undoubtedly their interest in this book, as yet unwritten, had much to do with overcoming their natural reluctance to bring out the collected short stories.

Cable's literary career had been in abeyance for several years, and the warm letters from Gilder and Boyesen early in 1878 gave new direction to his life. He wrote Boyesen to thank him, though he probably did not yet know the full extent of his help in winning acceptance for the short stories. He seemed to see no connection between the arrangements to issue a book of Creole tales and the sudden approval of his unwritten novel, and he was disturbed to realize that he could expect no income from the novel until it was finished. Having committed the publishers to Cable's future, Boyesen now wrote to bind the other party to the contracts he had engineered. He encouraged Cable by telling of his own struggles to support his dependents and compose his books in the hours lesser men had to devote to sleep. "God intended to make something very fine of both of us," he said, assuring Cable that his success was certain because "fame has already marked you for her own."

Anxious to win the promised success, Cable made adjustments of his office routines that let him apply his pen to fiction even though it had to continue, in some measure, to add figures in the counting room. Boyesen's assistance now took the form of suggestions about the title for the book of short stories and discussions of literary principles and the plot structure of the novel. His own early novels were traditional light romances, but he was turning toward Howellsian realism. His first reaction to Cable's projected novel was approval for its value as "a work in which the struggling forces of opposing civilizations crystalize & in which they find their enduring monument." Now he argued against contrived plots, strained coincidences, and surface description in favor of careful character development and an emphasis on situations which typified the culture being depicted. Cable agreed, but he inveighed against novels "that smell of the moral like very small houses do of the dinner that is cooking in the kitchen."

In the fall of 1878, Boyesen worried when his letters to Cable from Germany, where Boyesen had taken his bride for a visit, brought no response from New Orleans. Finally Cable wrote, on November 5, to detail the ravages of the plague that had visited the city that season, the worst yellow fever epidemic since 1853. It had not spared the crowded Cable home on Eighth Street. Among the first affected were two brothers-in-law, husbands of Mrs. Cable's sisters. Both the men roomed at the author's house, one of them having been hired as a counting room assistant to give Cable time to work on his novel. Other members of his household—his wife, four daughters, his son, and two colored servants—suffered attacks of varying severity. Good fortune and fine nursing saved all the immediate family except the boy, George. Another victim was Walter Cox, husband of Cable's sister Antoinette; his death added a penniless widow and three children to Cable's burdens. He moved the Coxes, his mother, and his sister Mary Louise to a house across the street from his cottage, where Mary Louise taught the children of the family and a few private pupils. Despite the family losses from the plague, Cable soberly told Boyesen that he thought

God had been good in sparing them from greater loss than they had received.

In preparing his stories for book publication, Cable heeded Boyesen's advice to avoid extensive revisions. After *Old Creole Days* appeared in May, 1879, Boyesen wrote in July to commend it and to suggest that in future printings the stories be arranged with a view to their relative merit rather than in the order of their magazine publication, a recommendation generally followed in the many reprintings of the volume. It sold well enough to make Boyesen's guarantee superfluous. Cable learned, as Boyesen had not intended he should, about the arrangement by which his friend had risked his money as well as his reputation in his behalf. The Southern author made no public acknowledgment of his indebtedness to Boyesen, though he paid tribute to other men who aided him. Before he died in 1895, Boyesen may have lost some of his regard for G. W. Cable as a person, but he had no cause to regret his part in contributing *Old Creole Days* and *The Grandissimes* to American literature.

ges Kookoo to believe he can learn, after fifteen years
ng, the secret of the chest, the rooms are taken by a
ne woman and her mulatto maid, a slave, who guard the
s zealously as the man had. 'Sieur George returns years
e war, accompanied by a tall Creole drinking companion
urts and wins the handsome woman. Regaining his rooms
e marriage, 'Sieur George continues to frustrate Kookoo's
about the trunk and reverts to the dissolute behavior
arly days.

day he comes home carrying an infant, the child of his
g companion and of "poor, robbed, spirit-broken and now
Madame." Soon the father dies too, and 'Sieur George
ne girl until she becomes of an age when it would
the proprieties for her to remain with him. Driven to
pping and to peeping through keyholes, Kookoo over-
is roomer lament that he had not done more for his
protégée, and he gives her a pious blessing as he tells
must leave him. As he speaks of his failures, he seems
y that the girl is related to him. When she tells him she
leave him, he, "having kept a good resolution all day,
couraged by the orphan's pitiful tones to contemplate
t senseless act he ever attempted to commit. He said to
bing girl that she was not of his blood; that she was
to him by natural ties; that his convenant was with her
e to care for his offspring; and though it had been poorly
might be breaking it worse than ever to turn her out
er so kind a world." Then, the paternal mask dropped,
her if she understands that parting could be avoided:
could be—my wife, dearie?"[1]
girl flees to her room and locks the door; and Kookoo, his
unsatisfied curiosity driving him to overcome his natural
ce, invades the apartment that night while 'Sieur George
, drunken stupor. When at last he gets his hands on the
ir trunk, he finds it "full, full, crowded down and running
l, of the tickets of the Havana Lottery." The Creole had
the trunk held treasure, not evidence of the disease
hich its owner had suffered for nearly fifty years. The
rning Kookoo watches the orphan steal from the house.
er sees her again, nor does 'Sieur George, though she
mfortable refuge nearby. Once from a distance she sees

CHAPTER 2

Creole Days in Old New Orleans

I *Aura of Bygone Days*

THE EARLIEST of the stories collected in *Old Creole Days*,
"'Sieur George," begins:

> In the heart of New Orleans stands a large four-story brick
> building, that has so stood for about three-quarters of a century.
> Its rooms are rented to a class of persons occupying them simply
> for lack of activity to find better and cheaper quarters elsewhere.
> With its gray stucco peeling off in broad patches, it has a solemn
> look of gentility in rags, and stands, or, as it were, hangs, about
> the corner of two ancient streets, like a faded fop who pretends
> to be looking for employment.

Thus Cable strikes the notes that resound in his later writing,
so much of it about New Orleans, the aura of a bygone day
hanging over the scene and diffusing the sharpness of the images.
Here is the rented room, the habitation of so many of his
characters. Here, too, is a class of persons who, even in the past,
looked to a remote time as the source of their respectability and
whose decline is symbolized by the physical decay of their
surroundings as well as hinted at by the author's suggestive
"solemn look of gentility in rags" and "faded fop who pretends
to be looking for employment." The impact of the passage is
rather a different thing than the specific statement; its effective-
ness lies in what is suggested rather than in what is denoted.
The technique is continued in the second paragraph.

> Under its main archway is a dingy apothecary-shop. On one
> street is the bazaar of a *modiste en robes et chapeaux* and other
> humble shops; on the other, the immense batten doors with
> gratings over the lintels, barred and bolted with masses of cob-

webbed iron, like the door of a donjon, are overhung by a creaking sign (left by the sheriff), on which is faintly discernible the mention of wines and liquors. A peep through one of the shops reveals a square court within, hung with many lines of wet clothes, its sides hugged by rotten staircases that seem vainly trying to clamber out of the rubbish.

Again the suggestion of olden times and of an exotic scene is achieved by an extremely skillful selection of details presented in such a way as to imply more than is stated. The French cultural background (already indicated by the story's title, with a special value deriving from the colloquial flavor of " 'Sieur") is established by *"modiste en robes et chapeaux"* and reinforced, as is the feeling of decadence and antiquity, by "donjon." "Cobwebbed" and "creaking" make this antiquity vivid to the reader's senses.

The physical point of view, the position from which the writer describes the scene at hand, has been announced, though it is to change with need as the story progresses. The very sentence which announces it reaffirms the author's omniscient angle of narration, apparent from the opening lines. Cable has closed in on the immediate scene of his narrative. Having begun with a general area, "the heart of New Orleans," and directed attention to a four-story building, he has moved to a vantage point from which it can be determined that the letters on a faded sign spell out "wines and liquors." His knowledge of the setting is not confined to what he can see at a given time and place, and his description is not free of value judgments, based on cultural prejudices, about his material. Omniscient, he knows that the sign was left by the sheriff, an official (of the shire) who represents an Anglo-Saxon rather than a French society.

Something is implied in these lines about the cultures at odds in New Orleans, the conflict between an amoral Latin tradition and puritanical Anglo-Saxon standards. There is a hint of the part indulgence in wines and liquors is to play in the story, and the reader is encouraged to infer that the narrative expresses disapproval of alcoholic beverages. The image with which the passage closes is indicative of concern because of the extent to which social conditions may prevent even the most aspiring citizen from scrambling "out of the rubbish" of his environment.

In this masterful introduction, Cable es[...] important for its atmosphere than its [...] that he is an acute, imaginative observ[...] his subject matter is partly that of a s[...] patronizing moralist.

Too often he is thought of as merel[...] recorder who found close at hand mat[...] stuff of fine literature. He used history[...] by it. The chronology we may piece ou[...] George" indicates that it is at least 18[...] ends; but, because the Civil War has [...] Cable blandly disregards that historic [...]

His material for this and other fictio[...] thing but several. Only superficially i[...] times. The action of the story begins [...] Mexican War, at a time when the fo[...] very fashionable neighborhood" and w[...] New Orleans." Both these virtues the [...] the time Cable chose to describe, in [...] stood in sorry reality at the corner of R[...] He chose to depict Creoles like those [...] neighborhood in his own time, not [...] there in its days of elegant respectabili[...] mediately following those quoted abov[...] sented as proprietors of fifth-rate sho[...] innumerable children. The wives are [...] women" in cotton gowns; the husban[...] warehouses, rent-collectors for the agen[...] have been laid up to dry in Paris, custo[...] and court clerks' deputies (for your se[...] seeker for little offices)." Adding an i[...] the most serious kind of injury, Cab[...] landlord of the building, as "an an[...] purity of blood."

Kookoo's curiosity is aroused by an [...] mysterious roomer keeps locked in hi[...] George, who is not a Creole and w[...] knows, often comes home exhibiting " [...] tions," but he never relaxes his gua[...] When 'Sieur George's sudden departu[...]

her former patron, now so destitute he must take his night's rest in the high grass of the prairies, but he does not succeed in finding her. He would like to "get from her the use of ten dollars for but three days," because he thinks he knows a "combination" that would bring him the fortune he has wasted his life pursuing.

"'Sieur George" has the standard ingredients of didactic melodrama. The plot is banal; the outcome is pathos, not tragedy. The characters of the main story are drawn from stock: the orphan, the wronged woman, the faithful servant, the drunkard, the gambler. At first 'Sieur George seems cast, uncertainly, as hero; then as villain; and at last as the victim of his compulsion. As social criticism the story is insipid, for it does not establish the viciousness of the state lottery by portraying the downfall of one exceptional man brought to grief by his addiction to this form of gambling. Yet, despite its weaknesses, the story is an arresting one because it is so adroitly told. Only when the trunk is opened is the reader disappointed to find so much genuine artistry wasted on so unworthy a tale. And much of that artistry lies in Cable's skill in shifting the angle of narration, alternating between omniscience and the limited consciousness and restricted physical position of Kookoo to give the attenuated story suspense and win the reader's temporary suspension of disbelief. Kookoo emerges as a vivid personality, the personification of the Creole milieu. It is the rendering of this milieu that is the real achievement of the narrative.

Cable's later fiction was sometimes criticized because Negro characters were given more favorable treatment than were Creoles. An anticipation of this characteristic may be seen in this first story. The young Creoles of the neighborhood speak of the mulatto slave who serves Madame as "confound' good lookin'," an appraisal somewhat more admiring than Cable's reference to the Creole wives as "passably good-looking." It does not follow, because Cable's picture of Creole character in this and other stories attains artistic excellence, that it is either just or generous.[2] In his early books, as in this first story, Cable represents the Creole as picturesque, but his description is loaded with sly ridicule and, sometimes, forthright scorn. For example, Kookoo is "old and wrinkled and brown, a sort of periodically animate mummy" who smokes cascarilla, wears velveteen, regards suggestions that he repair his decaying property as personal insults, and speaks *to himself* in droll broken English rather than in Creole-French. He is "intensely a coward." Cable's story covers a good many years, but he does not choose to show Kookoo at a more vigorous age or in a more attractive light. Moreover, when 'Sieur George astonishes the neighborhood by appearing in uniform, ready to depart for the Mexican War, the Creoles are incredulous; Cable says: "What to do or say or think they do not know; they are at their wits' ends, therefore well-nigh happy." They stand back deferentially while a German[3] proceeds to find out for them the explanation of the *Américain's* strange attire.

The story does not suggest that the dissolute 'Sieur George is a typical Anglo-Saxon. It does, however, encourage the assumption that Kookoo is representative of his race, and it indulges in some generalizations about "second-class" Creoles. No first-class Creoles figure in the story, an omission that lets readers infer there were none. This inference was not seriously challenged when Cable used Creoles as heroes and heroines in later works, because these characters were exceptions to the general pattern and attained nobility only as they rose above the traits Cable assigned to their society—a society he saw in terms of the contrary values of his own puritanical Protestant background. It was ironic that Cable should be a Sabbatarian in a city where stores and amusements operated as openly on Sunday as during the week. Cable disparaged Creole New Orleans because "Theatres, processions, dry-goods stores, government establishments, banks, hotels, and all spirit of enterprise were gone to Canal Street and beyond." Business success and the spirit of enterprise Cable admired all his life. Professional moralist and reformer as he was, and an ardent believer in the superiority of the Anglo-Saxon, Cable did well to depict in his stories much of the appeal of a culture with which he was basically out of sympathy.

II "Belles Demoiselles Plantation"

"Belles Demoiselles Plantation" is a repetition and extension of the narrative pattern he used for his first story. Again the title prepares the reader for the Gallic content of the tale, but it also has the added virtue of indicating that the subject is the aristocracy, not the second-class Creoles who provided atmosphere for " 'Sieur George." Again the pretense of sharing the sentiments of the Creole characters is a sly way of belittling their pretensions. The story concerns the De Charleu family, which is proud of a founding father who, on being recalled to France to explain the convenient loss of his account books, married a French gentlewoman, forgetting that he had left behind in Louisiana a Choctaw wife and children. Says Cable: "A man cannot remember everything!"

The protagonist is Colonel De Charleau, descendant of the original Count and his French wife. His every act is motivated by love for his seven beautiful daughters and his pride in his aristocratic lineage. De Charleau owns a mansion on the banks of the Mississippi, but he longs for a town house where his daughters may enjoy the delights of the social season in the New Orleans of 1820. He would like, also, to assemble in his own hands the scattered inheritance of his family. Part of that heritage, a decrepit business block in town, belongs to Injin Charlie, the Colonel's "extremely distant relative on the Choctaw side." The Colonel owes Charlie $180,000, a sum he can not pay and does not intend to try to pay. His ambition to buy the town property as a site for a summer home (how he could erect it is not clear) meets headlong the equal pride of Charlie, who wishes to retain the property as evidence of the justice of his claims to some portion of "fine" blood.

When an exchange of properties is proposed by Charlie, the Colonel agrees only because he discovers that the Mississippi is cutting into his land and will wash away his plantation (heavily mortgaged to Charlie) within three months. Honor—a trader's honor—requires that he bring Charlie to see the mansion before the bargain is sealed, but not that he reveal the fate in store for it. As the two men watch, the Mississippi crashes through the crevasse and sweeps away not only the mansion but the Colonel's daughters. The denouement is a sentimental deathbed scene: the dying Colonel repents his discreditable bargain and Injin Charlie, his loyal servitor during the long illness before death, eases his remorse by saying the bargain was never made.

In mock praise of De Charleu's pride in his genealogy, Cable says that a Creole "will not utterly go back on the ties of blood, no matter what sort of knots those ties may be." The Colonel has his virtues, but, even before he tries to defraud Injin Charlie, his vices outweigh them if one shares Cable's view that dueling, drinking, gambling, and dancing at the St. Philippe Street quadroon balls are vices. "Bitter-proud and penurious," De Charleu "loved nothing but himself, his name, and his motherless children." This aristocrat is no more honorable than drunken Injin Charlie or the "second-class" Creoles of " 'Sieur George."

That the plot of "Belles Demoiselles Plantation" is melo-dramatic cannot be denied. Much has been written about the vicious caprices of the great Mississippi which, in cutting new chanels, might wash away overnight just such a mansion as the Colonel's.[4] But the disappearance of the house with all its occupants in the view of a startled Injin Charlie and a horrified De Charleu—and just at the point in their conversation which leaves in doubt their intent to swap properties—is a badly strained coincidence. The incident does not, however, offend readers who seek symbols and analogues; they, remembering "The Fall of the House of Usher," may take the fall of the house of De Charleu as a symbol for Creole New Orleans engulfed by a river of energetic Anglo-Saxons. The maudlin close may also be explained, but not excused, as a bow to the conventions of periodical literature of the time. If the action of the story has its faults, the work as a whole is a remarkable stylistic achievement. Cable infuses the narrative with the flavor of a remote time and place, a quality that is recalled when the plot and characters are forgotten.

III *"Jean-ah Poquelin" and Other Stories*

With the exception of " 'Tite Poulette," the other tales compos-ing *Old Creole Days* need not be examined in detail in this study. The best of them, "Jean-ah Poquelin," is particularly suc-cessful in depicting a cosmopolitan old New Orleans in which an enervated Creole society finds itself falling under the dom-inance of a more enterprising American culture. Though it is set in the past—"when the Creoles were still kicking at such vile innovations as the trial by jury, American dances, anti-smuggling laws, and the printing of the Governor's proclamation in English"—the story is a vigorous picture of contending social forces. The scene moves away from the Vieux Carré; the technique turns from romance toward social criticism.

The story is significant, too, for its inclusion of a little man named White, the secretary of the board of a building and improvement company. This "mild, kind-hearted little man, who . . . had no fear of anything, unless it was the fear of being unkind," is the author's earliest projection of himself in fiction. Cable, whose Confederate enlistment papers described his complexion as dark, pointedly names his alter ego "White" and, naturally, he makes him an Anglo-Saxon. His status in the community is a modest one, in contrast with that of the more pretentious figures who personify the author in Cable's later works.

White is a functional character who lifts "his ineffectual voice" in an effort to prevent the persecution of Jean-ah Poquelin. Once an indigo planter, then a smuggler, then an African slave-trader, the old Creole is now a recluse tormented by superstitious Creoles and immigrants and hounded by aggressive American "interlopers." He is adamantly opposed to the plans of the new American government to drive a street through his marsh. "The scene in which old Poquelin confronts the Governor of Louisiana is one of the memorable ones in American literature."[5] When the street does go through, Jean-ah is hated because he neglects to build on his dried-up land. He is feared because the white figure seen on his property is assumed to be the ghost of his brother Jacques, who, having failed to return from the last Poquelin venture to the Guinea coast, is thought to have been murdered by Jean-ah. At last Cable achieves a tragic ending, not mere pathos, as the dead body of old Jean-ah is carried into the swamp by his black slave and Jacques, a leper.

In "Madame Délicieuse," unique among Cable's early tales in presenting only pure-blooded Creole aristocrats whose speech is not represented in broken English, the characters have no vices, only frailties enough to let Cable spin the web that entangles the lovers. Dr. Mossy, a mild-manered physician, has been disinherited by his father, General Villivicencio, because he is more devoted to his profession than to resisting the Americans who, by 1830, have replaced the Creole aristocrats as the dominant element in New Orleans. A temporary reconciliation ends abruptly when the physician fails to challenge an American newspaper editor to a duel in return for his derogatory comments about the General's decision to run for public office. Madame Délicieuse, a lovely widow whose principles are "not constructed in the austere Anglo-Saxon style, exactly (what need, with the lattice of the confessional not a stone's-throw off?)," cleverly resolves all the complications. She manages to reject the General's proposal of marriage without seriously offending him, forces his reconciliation with his son, and marries Dr. Mossy, who is no longer disinherited. Madame Délicieuse is typical of Cable's heroines, who often have more intelligence and strength of character than their male counterparts.

When Cable thought of calling his collected stories *Prose Idyls for Hammock and Fan,* he must have had in mind "Café des Exilés." This contrived tale is likely to please only the most undemanding and romantic reader, but it offers rewards for the student of Cable's work. Included in his description of the Spanish Creoles from Barbados, Martinique, San Domingo, and Cuba who were living in New Orleans as exiles in 1835 are aspersions on their claims of purity of blood. One of these refugees is Cable's villain, whose treachery foils the exiles' plot to ship arms to Cuba, and another is his beautiful heroine, but the hero is an Irish adventurer; whenever there are major characters who are not of Creole extraction in Cable's dramatis personae, the role of hero falls to one of them. In the romance of Galahad Shaughnessy and Pauline D'Hemecourt, Cable gives his blessing to what might be called a mixed marriage. The many mixed alliances in his fiction follow the pattern established in "Café des Exilés." Always the male partner belongs to a race commonly regarded by Americans at the time as superior to the race of the woman. A beautiful Creole girl may win the love of an Anglo-Saxon, or an octoroon may capture a male Creole, but the coin is never reversed. Inherent in this one-sided picture of mixed romance is a falsification of history (and human nature) and evidence that Cable's liberalism was not unblemished by conventional ideas of racial superiority.[6]

In "Café des Exilés" Cable added the Irish brogue to his stock in trade, and for "Posson Jone'" he mastered another speech pattern, that of a Baptist clergyman from West Florida. Because of its picture of a minister who falls victim to drink, "Posson Jone'" met widespread editorial objections. Today, when the sentimentality of some of the other stories of *Old Creole Days* makes them period pieces, the humor of this tale is still appealing. Some of the humor is supplied by the parson, some by Jules St.-Ange, an indolent young Creole who sees the naïve minister as an ideal victim for a confidence game. Jules's plan to appropriate for himself the church money the parson is carrying is defeated by the parson's slave, who fails, however, to prevent his master from getting drunk, inciting a riot at Cayetano's Circus, and spending a night in the *calaboza*.

Cable was himself a pious Presbyterian when he wrote the story, but he was sophisticated enough to ridicule the parson's narrow sectarianism and to put into the mouth of the Creole latitudinarian principles of the sort he came to hold later in life. New Orleans misfit though he was, Cable shows that he relishes the colorful mélange of races in his native city. Fine descriptive passages, firmly rooted in the details of local history, bring to life the vitality and variety of public entertainment for a heterogenous New Orleans population even less sedate and genteel than it was in Cable's own time.

> In the high upper seats of the rude amphitheatre sat the gayly decked wives and daughters of the Gascons, from the *metairies* along the Ridge, and the chattering Spanish women of the market, their shining hair unbonneted to the sun. Next below were their husbands and lovers in Sunday blouses, milkmen, butchers, bakers, black-bearded fishermen, Sicilian fruiterers, swarthy Portuguese sailors in little woollen caps, and strangers of the graver sort; mariners of England, Germany, and Holland. The lowest seats were full of trappers, smugglers, Canadian *voyageurs*, drinking and singing; *Américains*, too—more's the shame—from the upper rivers—who will not keep their seats, who ply the bottle, and who will get home by and by and tell how wicked Sodom is; broad-brimmed, silver-braided Mexicans, also, with their copper cheeks and bat's eyes, and their tinkling spurred heels. Yonder, in that quieter section, are the quadroon women in their black lace shawls . . . and below them are the turbaned black women. . . .

All the Creole stories are told in a series of dramatic episodes linked by passages of description or commentary that stress the exotic quality of the scene and intrude the personality of an author who manipulates his omniscience to contrive charming touches not unrelated to his own whimsical personality. The structure, artificial though it often is, creates an entertaining tension, a sense of mystery, a moment of sentimental climax. Didactic and moralistic elements are kept in the background, but the stories give enough history and social criticism to enable the reader to make inferences about issues far larger than those confronting the characters.

IV "'Tite Poulette"

That Cable had the capacity for greater depth of achievement than that of antiquarian and romancer, he showed in "'Tite Poulette." This story engages the elements of Louisiana culture with which he was most deeply concerned: the fact of slavery, as the historic phenomenon conditioning nearly all relations in the society; and the fact of caste, which was in Louisiana both the concomitant of slavery and its pervasive aftermath. Kristian Koppig, the young Dutch hero of "'Tite Poulette," is a recent immigrant to old New Orleans. (Cable was very conscious of being a Christian of German extraction. One branch of his family retained an earlier spelling of the name, Kable. Originally, in Würtemberg, it had been Kobell.) The beautiful women, apparently mother and daughter, whose humble quarters are across the street from his rented room arouse his interest. This becomes sympathy when he is told they are not white. Zalli, who affects the name Madame John, is "a palish handsome woman . . . fading," but "still of very attractive countenance, fine, rather severe features, nearly straight hair carefully kept, and that vivid black eye so peculiar to her kind." Her beauty is eclipsed by that of the fairer younger woman, "her form all grace, her carriage a wonder of simple dignity." Notwithstanding "the loose New Orleans morals of fifty years ago," the Creoles who admire her as she passes on the street attempt no greater liberty than "to take up the pet name, 'Tite Poulette."

Zalli's history is the common tragedy of the quadroon caste. Her white protector, Monsieur John, had tried to provide security for his mistress before he died, but Zalli and Poulette, now destitute, are unable to support themselves by embroidery and music lessons or by Madame John's reputation for excellence as a nurse. They are ever beaten back "by the steady detestation of their imperious patronesses." In desperation, Zalli becomes a paid dancer at the Salle de Condé. Koppig cannot keep himself from falling in love with Poulette or from offering the women assistance they feel it improper to accept. When Koppig goes to the ball to persuade Zalli, for the sake of her daughter's reputation, not to dance, he is set upon by the manager and his hirelings. Their blows and knife thrusts are accompanied by incredibly stilted dialogue. "That for yesterday." "That for 'Tite Poulette!" "And *that* for me!" The women nurse Koppig back to health in their apartment. When he tells Poulette of his love and asks her to be his wife, she reminds him that the law forbids them to marry. Madame John resolves the impasse by producing "sworn papers" as evidence that Poulette is not her daughter but the child of Spaniards.

Dialect was a popular feature of the literature of the time, and Cable was an exceptionally accurate recorder of the varied speech patterns he heard. It was his practice to force his Creole characters to speak the hated tongue of the *Américains* and to represent their Creole-French in broken English. The droll patois lends color to the stories, but, as Cable knew, it also gives the impression that Creoles were uncultured and semiliterate. In " 'Tite Poulette" the women, for whom Cable hoped to win the reader's full sympathy, have all the beauty, gentility, and nobility necessary to guarantee that sympathy. The conversation of Zalli and Poulette, whether in French or English, is represented as standard in grammar and enunciation. What they lose in quaintness, they gain in dignity. The Creole lads in the street may say of Poulette's age they "would give her about seventeen," but no such delightful idiom is permitted the heroines or the hero. Koppig speaks and writes very poor French, but Cable knew that to approximate in English the halting speech in which Koppig proposes to Poulette would be to make the love scene border on the ludicrous. Instead, Cable manages to suggest the quality of the language by having Koppig shift from "you" to "thou" in telling of his love, a device that emphasizes the pastoral tone and idyllic outcome of the story and invites comparison (already brought to mind by the interracial theme) with the Book of Ruth.

In Zalli's youth the quadroon balls, which Cable describes in " 'Tite Poulette" and elsewhere with considerable relish, were "decorously conducted" affairs at which white gentlemen met glamorous quadroon and octoroon women. Sometimes alliances were formed that lasted a lifetime. At the time of the story, however, the once select balls feature paid dancers and are patronized by rowdies. Zalli keeps Poulette away from the Salle de Condé and plans for her no "arrangement" of the sort her mother had once made for her with Monsieur John. She tries to persuade Poulette to promise not to reveal her fraction of Negro blood if a suitor, a gentleman, should ask her to marry him. Poulette refuses, unwilling to break the law prohibiting her from marrying a white man. Zalli protests: "the law is unjust." Earlier she has railed against the caste system; it is society she condemns, not herself, when she cries "*Sin* made me, yes." Koppig, a very proper, moral young man, had that sin in mind when he wrote his mother that New Orleans was a "wicked city." Cable's villain is not, therefore, the theater manager, "a smooth man, with his hair parted in the middle, and his cigarette poised on a tiny gold holder"—the man whom Koppig knows "as one knows a snake." The real culprit is society, whose villainy Zalli can thwart only by evading the laws that doom her caste to dishonor.

However the resolution of the story may satisfy the reader's emotions, it is a serious artistic weakness. When all the details of "'Tite Poulette" are considered, it is difficult to regard Zalli's claim that the girl is not her daughter as the truth. It seems rather a necessary and justifiable expedient. Since the reader cannot be certain, the story has a kind of ambiguity that was congenial to the author but incompatible with his purpose. (Cable told one of his daughters who asked if he would answer a question truthfully, "No. But I will promise not to lie to you."[7] She took this as evidence of her father's absolute devotion to truth, an interpretation of dubious validity.) The resolution of the story is ineffective even if Zalli's statement is accepted at its face value; it converts a piece of social criticism into an insipid fairy tale about a beautiful damsel whose right to marry the prince rests on the revelation that she is of royal birth, not on her human rights or personal worth.

Old Creole Days may be called, quite legitimately, a masterpiece of local color, an expression that praises its achievement and damns its limitations. In his next works, *The Grandissimes* and *Madame Delphine,* Cable moved away from the superficial genre he had helped to bring into vogue, in order to come to grips with the fundamental problems that had produced and still controlled the complex society which was his subject. These two books, products of his growing social consciousness and of his disciplined artistic maturity, are American classics.

CHAPTER 3

"Impassioned Advocate"

I *The Grandissimes*

LIKE ALL the best of Cable's fiction, *The Grandissimes*, which began its serial run in *Scribner's Monthly* in November, 1879, and was published in book form in 1880, is a blend of romance and realism. Never again did he achieve so perfect a combination of these elements, perhaps because he was not fully aware of the nature of the accomplishment. When he was campaigning for civil rights for Negroes, he said he meant to make *The Grandissimes* a political work, a study of the struggle he saw going on all around him in New Orleans. A few years later, when he had withdrawn from the race controversy and had come to believe that the primary function of fiction was to entertain, he described the novel as merely a traditional story of feuding families. Cable's basic plot line is always melodramatic. He had great difficulty in creating a convincing hero, and never conceived a noble protagonist who was not a wooden, posturing puppet. James M. Barrie praised his Creole women as too charming to be real, and William Dean Howells thought them as delightful creatures as any novelist had produced, but Cable's heroines are hardly more real than his heroes. His plots and his leading characters, superficially exotic but fundamentally identical with the stereotyped, genteel figures of conventional popular literature, are expressions of the romantic side of Cable's personal character. All the greatness of *The Grandissimes* must be attributed to the G. W. Cable who was social critic, historian, and reformer. The exciting minor characters, the vivid re-creation of the fullness of life in a bygone era, the incisive social commentary—these are really the body of the novel and the sources of its strength. Some of Cable's short stories deal almost entirely in what Granville Hicks has called the "picturesque trifles" of local color.[1] But *The Grandissimes* is what Boyesen predicted it would be when he saw Cable's preliminary sketch: a penetrating study of a society torn by conflicting cultural traditions.

The two heroes are symbolic of the contrasting civilizations whose opposition was heightened by the transfer of Louisiana from France to the United States in 1803, the year with which the novel is concerned. One of these heroes, perhaps an answer to the charge that Cable had ignored the finer Creole types, is Honoré Grandissime; the other is Joseph Frowenfeld, an immigrant who is "American by birth, rearing, and sentiment, yet German enough through his parents." He is "German enough" to be Cable's alter ego, a more fully developed Kristian Koppig, but he is too idealistic and alien to Southern principles to represent Louisiana Americans, who have Dr. Charlie Keene as their spokesman. The Creole mother and daughter who are Cable's heroines speak the quaint patois he had used so skillfully in his stories. When he revised the novel in 1883 he eliminated some of the patois in the conversations of Honoré Grandissime and Frowenfeld, although Frowenfeld's convenient ignorance of French makes it necessary for the Creoles to address him in English.

Honoré is another reminder of Cable's habit of censuring the Creole male, for Honoré's nobility is in direct proportion to his deviation from the Creole practices and his rejection of the Creole principles the author indicts throughout the book. Even at the beginning of the novel, Honoré has strayed from Creole traditions to become a merchant, competing in the Yankee world of business that the Creoles scorned but which Cable venerated all his life. In Honoré's hands are the business affairs of one of the feuding families, the powerful Grandissimes. The other family, the De Grapions, is represented by Aurora and Clotilde Nancanou, mother and daughter. Aurora's estate was lost at the gaming table and her husband's life in the duel that followed, both losses for which she holds the Grandissimes responsible. Honoré's dilemma, complicated by his love for Aurora, is whether or not to make restitution to the women against the wishes of all the Grandissimes and at a time when the clan's financial position is endangered by the advent of Yankee rule.

To Frowenfeld, who has heavier burdens than Honoré and bears them with a fortitude that wins the Creole's admiration, the problem is academic; he refuses to consider any course of action except one based on moral grounds. A few days after he arrives in New Orleans his parents and sisters die of yellow fever; his life is saved (as was Koppig's) by the devoted nursing[2] of a lovely young woman whose identity Frowenfeld does not know. So deserving a young man as Frowenfeld and so beautiful a young woman as Clotilde Nacanou are not, in a romantic plot, to be kept apart permanently. The discovery that Clotilde was the nurse dissolves the tissue of circumstances that has kept this pair separated. At the close of the novel the two sets of lovers are united, the feud ends, and the material fortunes of all are assured.

Frowenfeld, the inflexibly high-minded *raisonneur*, is both a conscious and unconscious personification of changes in Cable's attitudes since the writing five years earlier of " 'Tite Poulette." Like Kristian Koppig, Frowenfeld is an alien to the world of the Vieux Carré and the American South; unlike Koppig, Frowenfeld does not accommodate his principles to those of his adopted home. Koppig learns to share Louisiana's professed "horror of mixed blood," and, though he says Poulette's "hidden blemish" would not be detected by one in a hundred suitors if she were in Holland, he struggles to avoid falling in love with the girl; Frowenfeld, on the other hand, says the mixture of blood that makes a quadroon scorned "is to me nothing—nothing." Koppig deplores the moral laxity of the city, but he accepts the prevailing racial attitudes. For trying to protect the two women he pities, he is beaten and stabbed. But Frowenfeld, who actively advocates reform and campaigns for all the oppressed, is martyred by the whole community. Frowenfeld is the image of the man Cable was becoming. His fate at the hands of his neighbors is a prediction of the rejection Cable was to experience as successive books and articles traced the course of his wanderings from the prescribed narrow path the South insisted was the high road of virtue and necessity.

II *Anatomy of Southern Society*

As late as 1927, Robert Underwood Johnson, perhaps influenced by his editorial responsibilities for the serialization, said *The Grandissimes* was the greatest novel written by an American and one that ranked with the finest fiction of the world. Such praise was not uncommon; Howells, too, called the book one of the greatest American novels. Great it is, but its excellence does not lie in its main plot, the story of Creole Montagues and Capulets. Only when this frail skeleton is fleshed out with minor characters, historical background, social commentary, and minor plots does the final product become the distinguished creation that Edmund Wilson calls "the first full length installment of Cable's anatomy of Southern society."[3]

Perhaps the mildest charge that Creoles made against Cable was that in depicting them in fiction he confined his efforts to generalizing the unrepresentative and uncomplimentary exception. If some of the stories of *Old Creole Days* support this contention, *The Grandissimes* does not. In it Cable uses a wide variety of Creoles of all types and conditions: young and old, rich and poor, patrician and commoner, sophisticated and naïve, cruel and benevolent, industrious and indolent, charming and offensive. There are Creoles of unquestioned pure blood whose ancestors were French or Spanish aristocrats;[4] others have lineages which include Choctaw squaws or plebeian maidens—*filles à la cassette*—sent from France in the eighteenth century to become the wives of soldiers, or Paris street girls sent earlier for the same purpose.[5]

The Creoles were only one element in the cosmopolitan city made American by the Louisiana Purchase, and Cable does not neglect the others. Because of his German ancestry and his refusal to accept the standards of his new home, Frowenfeld represents the immigrants, though such absolute nobility as his could hardly be typical of any group. An anticipation of the physician Cable features in his second novel, Dr. Charlie Keene speaks for the Americans, whose arrival in numbers and whose authority create the conflict of cultures which underlies so much of the action of the narrative. He is like Cable in admiring Creole women, tolerating the men, and condescending to Latin patterns of life. There the likeness ends. A "Creolized *Américain*," Dr. Keene does not disapprove of slavery or caste; he would be content to modernize the social order by stimulating commercial enterprise, professional efficiency, and industrial expansion. This was the program many of Cable's contemporaries advocated for the New South, a program Cable thought provided no solution for the basic inequalities of personal status and opportunity that prevented the South, more than any other section of the country, from attaining the democratic ideals of the nation's founders. But Cable was not ready to attack the New South's doctrines directly. Frowenfeld respects Dr. Keene, treating him as an equal with a right to his opinions, though the physician's attitude toward the Creoles is that of a missionary bringing the message of "higher morality." But Cable's puritanical hero was as much out of sympathy with the American New South that Dr. Keene hoped for as he was with old Creole Louisiana. Only in the New England of an earlier day would Frowenfeld have felt at home.

In a novel of the scope of *The Grandissimes*, Cable could hardly ignore the quadroon caste, whose peculiar position he had touched upon in the short stories. There are two important quadroons in the book, both departures from the types the author had presented previously. One of them, Cable's most detailed portrait of a male quadroon, is the namesake and half brother of Honoré Grandissime. He neglects to designate himself as a free man of color, as the law requires, by writing "f.m.c." after his signature, so the duplication of names gives opportunity for mistaken identity to complicate the plot. He also serves as a device to let Cable give expression, through Frowenfeld, to his opinions about what Negro leaders might do to help their race. Although one critic thinks the relationship of the two Honoré Grandissimes is a token of Cable's recognition of the interdependence of the two races in the South,[6] the quadroon, who explicitly refuses to be an advocate of any but his own personal and hopeless cause, symbolizes nothing but Cable's addiction to pathos. The half brothers were educated together in Paris (though Cable permits the inference that the quadroon is semiliterate while the Creole is a cultured man), but they are kept apart in New Orleans by the code of the community. The quadroon rises to some dignity at crucial moments in the novel, and he finally asserts his right to the name he bears when his money makes possible the return of the Nancanou estate without impoverishing the Grandissimes. His fate is suicide in France after his companion, Palmyre Philosophe, persists in her refusal to marry him.

Palmyre is the direct opposite of the refined, delicate, dependent young women of her caste whom Cable had drawn in the past. A barbaric, feline beauty, her love is not genteel expedience; her hatred is implacable. This woman, like all her caste, faced "what certainly was to her an unmerciful world." Though "she had stood all her life with dagger drawn" to protect herself, she is not content with defense; she would like nothing better than to teach her whole people—not merely her caste—insurrection. A priestess of *voudou*, she works a love spell for Aurora Nancanou, not knowing it is designed to win Creole Honoré Grandissime, the very man who is the object of her own unrequited passion. Palmyre's baleful arts torment the superstitious Creole patriarch who is her principal enemy, but it is the knife of the quadroon Honoré that causes his death.

III *Negro Problem*

Cable had no doubt that the fundamental problem of American public life was the presence of the Negro. In dealing with quadroons and octoroons, as numerous as they were in New Orleans, Cable had touched in his short stories only the periphery of the main issue: slavery. Many quadroons and octoroons were technically free and enjoyed a relatively privileged status; they owned slaves and other property, and they were able to acquire an education and a degree of personal security.[7] Understandably, they tended to accept—rather than to rebel against—the South's peculiar institution, and they did not generally identify themselves with the Negro masses. Yet many writers had seen the quadroon as an ideal subject for melodrama or as a means of stirring antislavery sentiment, as witness Longfellow's "The Quadroon Girl" (1842) and Frederick Law Olmstead's description of the liaisons between the women of this caste and upperclass white men in *A Journey in the Seaboard Slave States* (1856), a work that anticipated Cable's rendering of Acadian and Creole speech. The glamorous, tragic quadroon was established as a familiar stereotype long before Cable began to write.

From the point of view of sentiment, though not of logic, it was commonly supposed that the evils of slavery increased in direct proportion to the quantity of "white blood" in the slave's veins. Dion Boucicault capitalized on this belief when he used Mayne Reid's novel, *The Quadroon* (1856), as the basis for his sensational drama of life in Louisiana, *The Octoroon*. By cutting his heroine's "Negro blood" in half, he doubled her popular appeal; *The Octoroon* filled theaters in all the major cities of the Union during the first years of the Civil War. Even Harriet Beecher Stowe, the little woman Lincoln said brought on that war, thought a fair skin heightened the pathos of the slave, and so she added Cassy and George Harris to *Uncle Tom's Cabin* and Lizette and Harry Gordon to *Dred*. Cable was never so irrational as to suppose the sufferings of the quadroon more acute than those of the black masses; and he was never guilty of depicting Negroes of mixed blood as torn by inner conflicts, their white blood allegedly making them aspire for a virtue their black blood prevents them from attaining. His quadroons and octoroons, their tragedy the proscriptions of a caste society, are the most celebrated in American literature. He does not confine himself, however, to these romantic racial types. In the total body of his works he portrays a wide range of Negro types and experience, a fact many critics fail to acknowledge. There are in *The Grandissimes* two notable black characters who do much to make the novel a trenchant indictment of slavery.

Although the main events occur within one year, the action covers a much longer period, going as far back as 1673, the year when the Indian maiden was born whose later choice of a De Grapion suitor began the feud between the two great Creole families. Crucial to the main plot is the story of Bras-Coupé, who died eight years before Frowenfeld's arrival in New Orleans. A giant Jaloff prince, Bras-Coupé was brought to slavery in America on "the good schooner *Egalité*." (The irony Cable repeats later with mention of another slave ship, "the schooner *Freedom*.") Bras-Coupé accepts slavery, but not the idea of inferiority or the indignity of manual labor. He submits only when Palmyre is promised him as a wife, an arrangement agreeable neither to her nor to the Creoles whose blood she bears. At the wedding his first drink of wine makes the African forgetful of his place. Bras-Coupé fells his master with one blow of his fist, places a *voudou* curse on the plantation, and flees to the swamp. His course wreaks havoc on his enemies, while he eludes all efforts to capture him. Made bold and irresponsible by another encounter with drink, he joins the slave dancers in

Congo Square, where a noose is dropped over his head. In accordance with the *Code Noir*, the severe regulations by which both the French and Spanish rulers of old Louisiana hoped to prevent slave uprisings, Bras-Coupé is lashed, his ears are cut off, and he is hamstrung. A priest asks the dying slave, who has finally lifted the curse, if he knows where he is going. Bras-Coupé answers, " 'To—Africa'—and was gone."

Cable had written this story several years earlier and had tried to publish it in the periodicals, but editors found "Bibi," as it was then called, too "distressful" for their readers. It remains a separate story, two chapters long, within the novel, but it is woven inextricably into the main narrative. There are many scattered references to Bras-Coupé, who had chosen his name, meaning the Arm Cut Off, to indicate the importance of his loss to his tribe: "all Slavery is maiming," Cable adds. The story is a magnificent assault on the despicable *Code Noir* and on the "mental reservation" that Cable says is the Black Code of his own time. At the very outset of the story he condemns Bras-Coupé's enslavement: "He that made men's skins of different colors, but all of one blood, hath entered the same upon His book, and sealed it to the day of judgment." This equalitarian philosophy Cable had not found in the Louisiana documents and traditions he studied, though these offered abundant details of the horrors of the middle passage and accounts of Africans who chose death or mutilation rather than submit to slavery. His research provided enough analogues to justify the story. It is unlikely that he knew Mrs. Afra Behn's novel, *Oroonoko: The History of the Royal Slave* (1688), which closes with the black hero calmly smoking a pipe as his Irish executioner cuts off his organs, his ears, his nose, and one arm. He dies without a groan or a reproach when the other arm is hacked away.

As stirring a figure as he is, Bras-Coupé is not Cable's most significant agent for his attack on the oppression of the black man by the white South. During the half of his life that Cable spent in Massachusetts, where he regularly took part in the local G.A.R. Memorial Day observances, he was thought of as a Southerner in New England; but by the time he wrote *The Grandissimes* the New Orleans author had become, in spirit, a New Englander in the South. Two years after it was published he said in a letter that he had never felt at home until he visited the North, and he sent "Blessings on the day when Harriet Beecher Stowe was born."[8] He knew the social purpose of *The Grandissimes* could not be accomplished by showing exceptional victims of slavery, whether they were beautiful, fair-skinned women or Africans of regal birth and bearing. When Shakespeare's Othello, who fetched his life "from men of royal siege," told Desdemona of being "taken by the insolent foe and sold to slavery," he won her heart, his hardships and nobility overcoming her distaste for his complexion; but he did not make her an abolitionist. To complete his arraignment of the Old South of lashings and the New South of lynchings, Cable had to employ a figure to represent the black masses. In conceiving Clemence, an old black woman who is the slave of quadroon Honoré Grandissime and the confederate of Palmyre, he created one of the most realistic Negro characters in American literature. Cable's Clemence has little in common with Mrs. Stowe's sentimentalized, atypical Uncle Tom or the static Uncle Remus of Joel Chandler Harris. Though she has a relatively minor role in Cable's novel, Clemence is not unworthy of comparison with Jim, the slave Mark Twain's genius provided as foil and companion for the immortal Huck Finn.

Because Clemence was reared in Virginia, where she saw her mother sold at auction, she speaks the English dialect of the Southern Negro, but she uses also the patois of the Creole slaves. Her children are scattered in field gangs and Grandissime households. In the mornings Clemence sells rice cakes in the Rue Royale; in the evening ginger cakes are her merchandise; at night she secretly carries to the plantation of Palmyre's enemy the *voudou* charms that terrify the old Creole aristocrat. When Clemence dispenses her wares with equal aplomb to members of the Spanish guard, to Governor Claiborne's Yankee soldiers, to Creole priests and loungers, she adapts her speech and manners to the differing attitudes of her customers. Her sharp, wry humor is often audacious. Dr. Keene, who suffers defeat whenever he crosses swords with the *marchande des calas*, calls her "a thinker," and Cable says she has "made a life study of herself and her conditions." Aware that there is no chattel slavery in Europe, Clemence asks slyly why Louisiana whites praise the state of society abroad. When Dr. Keene says the slaves are "the happiest people under the sun," she is quick to deny the canard. He insists, "you niggers don't know when you are happy." "Dass so, Mawse—*c'est vrai, oui,*" she replies, "we donno no mo'n white folks!"

The Creoles do not fail to note the presumption beneath the old woman's bantering manner. One night, when she is caught in a steel trap on the Grandissime land, she has on her person a damning wax image in a coffin-shaped black box. The young men of the family gather at the edge of the swamp, and she sees she is in danger of more than a whipping. As a noose is slipped over over her head she begs—demands—that she be released: "You ain't got no mo biznis to do me so 'an if I was a white 'oman!" Some of the close kinsmen of the absent Honoré Grandissime let the strangling woman down from the tree branch. Other members of the family tell the old slave to run for her life. As she runs from the Creoles, who laugh to see her "scuttling and tripping and stumbling," a shot rings out. She falls to the ground, dead.

When Frowenfeld decides to become an apothecary in the exotic city of his adopted residence, he finds himself overwhelmed for a while by its "atmosphere of hints, allusions, faint unspoken admissions, ill-concealed antipathies, unfinished speeches, mistaken identities and whisperings of hidden strife." This is the atmosphere of the novel itself. Some readers suppose there is nothing beneath it, but Cable intended his story of olden times to explain why "Louisiana has grown up so out of joint." Many of his contemporaries saw that he had salted it with such analysis and forthright condemnation of both modern Dixie and the Louisiana of earlier times as to make himself, as James M. Barrie said, an "impassioned advocate of the black man."[9] As Frowenfeld becomes acclimated he concludes that he is living in a dangerously defective society, one "unprepared and disinclined to follow the course of modern thought" and "violently determined to hear no discussion" of its peculiar problems.

To the stunned Nancanou ladies he acknowledges that the new American government may someday abolish slavery. "But there is a slavery that no legislation can abolish—the slavery of caste. That, like all the slaveries on earth, is a double bondage.

And what a bondage it is which compels a community, in order to preserve its established tyrannies, to walk behind the rest of the intelligent world." It is Creole law that kills Bras-Coupé, it is a Creole mob that murders Clemence; but Cable points out that in his own day "almost all the savagery that can justly be charged against Louisiana must—strange to say—be laid at the door of the *Américain*." Southerners were to say of Cable what one outraged Creole says of Frowenfeld: "He has given us good reason half a dozen times, with his too free speech and his high moral whine, to hang him with the lamp-post rope!"

CHAPTER 4

On the Platform

I *Madame Delphine*

C ABLE DID NOT make the mistake of dodging the issue he had raised in " 'Tite Poulette" when he used the same basic plot a second time in *Madame Dephine*. Published in installments in *Scribner's Monthly* and as a separate book in 1881, this novella is the *pièce de résistance* in most subsequent editions of *Old Creole Days*. It has a high seriousness and a breadth of tolerance that is lacking in the shorter Creole stories. Except for a reference to "that significant fungus, the Chinaman" and a slur on *gens de couleur*, Cable indulges in no patronizing generalizations, no whimsical intrusions. There is abundant dialect, spoken by all the characters, but it is not used for comic effect and is replaced by standard English in the most serious episodes. Though the story takes place "sixty years ago and more," Cable describes the scene as it exists in "architectural decrepitude" in his time, an approach that serves to confirm the "truth" of the action rather than to rob it of vitality. There is verification, too, in the encyclopedic knowledge of local history the author demonstrates, knowledge that is authority for his judgments. Most important, what had been pity in " 'Tite Poulette" becomes in *Madame Delphine* real compassion for the plight of womanhood suffering a denial of basic rights by tradition and law.

Madame Delphine is in better circumstances than was her counterpart, Madame John, because her "protector"—an American, not a Creole—has left her property. When he died, his relatives took the daughter Madame Delphine had borne him, but once Olive is grown she sails to join her mother. The ship encounters the forces of a noted pirate, Ursin Lemaitre-Vignevielle (modeled on Jean Laffite), remarkable for his "courtesy and gentility." When he boards the vessel, he is so struck by the beauty of the girl that, in exchange for her Bible, he gallantly obeys her command to leave the ship unmolested. This is all antecedent action; at the time the story opens Vignevielle has abandoned piracy and smuggling to become a benevolent banker in his native New Orleans, where he wanders the streets in hope of finding the unidentified girl who had converted him.

The girl, as Cable describes her, would have converted any sentient male. "From throat to instep she was as white as Cynthia. Something above the medium height, slender, lithe, her abundant hair rolling in dark, rich waves back from her brows and down from her crown, and falling in two heavy plaits beyond her round, broadly girt waist and full to her knees, a few escaping locks eddying lightly on her graceful neck and her temples. . . ." When Vignevielle does find her and learns she returns his love, he determines to marry the girl even if they must settle in France where no law prohibits their alliance. To break the engagement, Vignevielle's relatives first try to convince Olive that he is crazy, and then they threaten to turn him over to the government agents who are seeking him; but Madame Delphine overcomes the relatives' hostility and makes the marriage possible when she produces "evidence" that Olive is not her daughter. Later, in the confessional of Père Jerome, the noble Creole priest who is Cable's spokesman in the story,[1] Delphine admits she fabricated the evidence and swore a false oath to validate it. The closing line is Père Jerome's, as he holds the dead woman in his arms: "Lord, lay not this sin to her charge!"

With this story Cable kicked up a hornet's nest—or kept the hornets buzzing that he had stirred up about a year earlier with *The Grandissimes*. Though he set the tale in the past, when "the free quadroon caste was in its golden age," it had very damaging implications for the present. Delphine and Olive, Cable made clear, were not unique. The quadroons and octoroons of old New Orleans had been made famous by the many accounts of "their faultlessness of feature, their perfection of form, their varied styles of beauty—for there were even pure Caucasian blondes among them—their fascinating manners, their sparkling vivacity, their chaste and pretty wit, their grace in the dance, their modest propriety, their taste and elegance in dress." How many of these Olives, by one deception or another, had brought their taint of Negro blood—imperceptible but legally damning—

into some aristocratic Creole family? How many contemporary Creoles, even those most adamant in asserting their purity of blood, had, unknowingly, an Olive in one generation or another of their proud ancestry? (In " 'Tite Poulette," in which there is no proof the girl the hero marries is colored, that hero is a Dutchman and a projection of the author. In *Madame Delphine*, in which a marriage takes place between a white man and an acknowledged octoroon, Cable makes the man a Creole.) Cable had not hesitated to speak about the ignominious origin of some Creole families, and in *The Grandissimes* he makes much ado about their tangled blood lines. He gave his New Orleans neighbors of French and Spanish ancestry additional offense by making the colored heroines of *Madame Delphine* the epitome of beauty and nobility, effectively dramatizing their plight, and winning for them and their descendants the sympathetic admiration of the nation's readers. The story may have the patina of a scrapbook memento faded by the passing years, but it has also the immediacy of a report from a current newspaper.

II   *Cable Goes North*

Most of Cable's friends advised him against attempting to derive his entire income from belles-lettres, but H. H. Boyesen, responding to Cable's premature announcement that he had decided on this course, encouraged him in his letter of September 5, 1880. Cable's circumstances had improved considerably over the past two or three years. *Old Creole Days* received favorable reviews and national attention, but Cable's income from the first edition was inconsequential so he remained at his counting-house desk and wrote when he could, sometimes with one of his children on his lap. The publishers granted generous terms for *The Grandissimes*, both as a serial and as a book. Cable drew a $500 advance when the revised early chapters were approved in March of 1879, a precedent he was to rely on—or to abuse—for the rest of his life. Though he periodically flirted with other firms, he was essentially loyal to the friends he made at Scribner's, who responded with support at ebb tides throughout his career. They granted him a $500 bonus because of the excellence of early installments of *The Grandissimes*, and they raised the rate of pay for his magazine contributions.

The death of Cable's friend and employer, William C. Black, late in 1879, tended to cut his ties with the countinghouse; but a more positive factor in freeing Cable from a clerical occupation was the appearance of Colonel George E. Waring, who visited New Orleans early in 1880 to collect data for the Tenth Census. Waring read *Old Creole Days* on the train, admired it, sought out Cable, and appointed him as an assistant. The information Cable sent Waring over the next fourteen months brought a steady income of $100 each month, and Waring's energetic interest in advancing his literary career brought prospects of additional money from writing. Moreover, Cable's research proved to be a long-range investment which provided him with information and notes he used to advantage in the future. The manuscript he wrote for Waring amounted to a history of New Orleans, from the founding to the Civil War, supplemented by a study of the regions of Louisiana occupied by the Acadians. This latter data he obtained by revisiting the country in which he had served as chain bearer for a surveying expedition after the war, when a severe attack of malaria put an end to thoughts of adopting engineering as a profession.

Cable's announcement that he planned to devote himself exclusively to literature pleased Boyesen, who had resigned his Cornell professorship for the same purpose. Now a resident of New York, Boyesen urged Cable to fulfill his "vague intention" of visiting that city. The visit took place a week later, in September, 1880, when Boyesen and Cable met for the first time during what was Cable's second trip to New York.

On his first, in July, 1875, he had arrived by boat from Havana, anxious to meet the editors who had helped him perfect the stories published in *Scribner's Monthly*. He had met Gilder, had toured the city with Frank R. Stockton, and had written home proudly of encounters with "two or three of the nabobs . . . in their splendid villas."[2] He may have been quite at ease, but his hosts found it awkward to entertain a man who did not smoke or drink at dinner and who thought the theater sinful. Cable's brief exposure to the North was enough to make a permanent appeal and to help him to see the South, as Boyesen did, as a kind of wasteland. Most gratifying was the sense of acceptance by men whose status and talent captured his imagination and fed his ambition.

His visit of 1880 was more consequential than the first. With *Old Creole Days* in print, *The Grandissimes* running as a serial, and *Madame Delphine* accepted for publication, Cable was a minor celebrity, not merely a promising new writer of short stories. He was entertained by the editors and assistants with whom he had crossed swords over passages in his works, and, exercising the full force of his personality, he made them his friends. So pleasant was this second visit to New York that he planned another for the following summer and, when the time came, decided that the whole family should have a taste of life in the North. (His wife, who had borne five children from 1870 to 1879, suffered severely from the humid Louisiana summers. Cable once wrote his mother of the burden his wife's "feeble frame" placed upon him. A periodic victim of poor health, Louise Cable benefited from the change of climate as much as her husband did from the change of scene.) Friends arranged for room and board for Mrs. Cable and the children at a farmhouse in Franconia, New Hampshire, where Cable deposited them in June, 1881, before returning to New York for another session with his friends and publishers.

The business that brought him to the East worked out very much to his advantage. In January, 1880, he had written Robert Underwood Johnson, the Scribner's editor who guided *The Grandissimes* into print, that he was ready to write another novel. A year later, Waring obtained an offer of $3,500 for book and serial rights to the projected work from James R. Osgood, a Boston publisher. Cable, who learned rapidly, managed to improve this arrangement when he settled the matter that summer in New York. Osgood won the book rights. A new firm, headed by Cable's friend Roswell Smith and composed of key staff members from *Scribner's Monthly*, paid $3,500 for the serial rights, $1,000 of it in advance. Cable contrived to avoid seriously offending Charles Scribner, who published all his important later books.

To judge by the letters to his family recording the highlights of his activities in New York, Newport, Boston, Concord, and Hartford, the social triumphs of this visit most delighted Cable. He took obvious pleasure in the travel itself—"the sort of excitement you know I like"[3]—and in establishing friendships with the prominent people he met. Among those he mentioned in letters notable for name-dropping were the Gilders, Waring, Charles Scribner, John Hay, Osgood, Harriet Beecher Stowe, Roswell Smith, Charles Dudley Warner, and Joseph Twitchell. He visited William Dean Howells at Belmont. Mark Twain and his wife made a special trip to meet him and, like Howells, found him captivating. Cable was honored on every hand; when he took the train for the South, he did so with the feeling that the greatest holiday in his life had ended. He wrote his wife and children from New Orleans that they must derive all the benefit they could from the stay among the Yankees and must be tolerant of what might seem strange ways: "remember we belong to nothing less than the whole human race and . . . these people are our brethren."[4]

He resumed work on his census study for Waring and, on June 29, submitted the report he had prepared as secretary of the grand jury investigating New Orleans jails and asylums. He had studied prisons and asylums in the East that summer, and what he saw at home and on his visit convinced him that the institutions in the Crescent City were badly in need of reform.

That fall, with several publishers competing for his work and urging literary projects upon him, Cable at last made the break with his clerical career which a year earlier he had told Boyesen was imminent. Later he was mistakenly to recall the decisive act of resignation as occurring only two or three months after the death of William C. Black; actually almost two years separated the two events. In any case, Cable was now free of the routines of the countinghouse and wholly dependent on his writing, or associated pursuits, for the support of his large family.

In January, 1882, Joseph Pennell came to New Orleans to prepare illustrations for the history of the Creoles which Cable composed as a revision of the census report he wrote for Waring. Cable found the artist a room in the French Quarter, guided his tours of the city, and introduced him to people who could aid his work. Pennell was enchanted by Cable's New Orleans, half of it Creole and half American, with Canal Street serving as the dividing line. His only disappointment was that the author, whom he regarded as the only American who knew the Creoles, was so roundly hated that he could not present his visitor to Creoles of the better class. Creoles had voiced strenuous objection to his work from the very beginning, but their disapproval Cable regarded as unimportant because, he told his publisher, they did not buy books. Creole indignation took extreme form in a reprehensible work by poet-priest Adrien Rouquette, *Critical Dialogue between Aboo and Caboo on a New Book; or, a Grandissime Ascension.* The scurrilous attack gave Cable's new friends some concern for his safety. Roswell Smith thought *Madame Delphine* was Cable's prayer for those who hated him, and he believed the moral he read between the lines of the story placed his friend's life in danger in the South.

III   *Adverse Critics*

George E. Waring conceded, in an article published in February, 1882, that Creoles resented Cable's writing, but he said he thought their attitude was becoming less hostile. On the contrary, resentment increased with the publication of the work Pennell came to New Orleans to illustrate. That work appeared as a series of articles in *Century Magazine,* beginning with the issue for January, 1883, and, after further revision, as *The Creoles of Louisiana* in 1884. Cable's hope that his history would placate those who felt he had dealt unfairly with the Creoles was foolish, for the book exhibited the same patronizing tolerance evident in his fiction. The fact that it offered no criticisms not mentioned by earlier historians, some of them Creoles, did nothing to abate Creole anger. In content, style, and moral point of view, the book parallels Cable's other pictures of old Louisiana and previews his impending campaign to win civil rights for the Negro. It shows his grasp of the significance of men and events, his interest in the principles of government, his addiction to didacticism and reform. Although Cable could not be in sympathy with an aristocratic Catholic culture he considered deficient in moral rectitude, he made *The Creoles of Louisiana* a creditable work, both as literature and history. It has brought him the respect of modern historians; it contributed to his reputation as an authority on a unique section of the country; but it won him no Creole friends.

The Creoles were not Cable's only adverse critics in the South, Waring said: "His frank and manly treatment of the peculiar problems of his native city has not failed to arouse a certain feeling of antagonism."[5] Joel Chandler Harris, writing under the name "Anne Macfarland," rebuked his fellow Southerners for their "hot criticism and social ostracism" of the author of *The Grandissimes*.[6] Unlike most admirers of the Creole stories, Harris hoped Cable would write about his own times. It was clear that Cable felt about New Orleans as he said Frowenfeld did: he was uncomfortable "among a people whose conventionalities were so at variance with his own door-yard ethics." Southern animosity was tempered by pride in Cable's national reputation as an author and by the supposition that his principal attack was aimed at slavery—a defunct institution. Southerners felt that Cable's portrait of Creoles was basically accurate; they did not see, or did not find disturbing, that it was also unsympathetic and uncomplimentary. But when Cable's social criticism moved away from the past and toward the present, Southerners outdid the Creoles in heaping abuse on him.

Cable was not yet regarded as a renegade when Mark Twain and James R. Osgood came to visit him in New Orleans in April, 1882. Twain was planning to make a book of the series of articles, "Old Times on the Mississippi," which he had published in 1875, and he wished to refresh his memories of the river. Cable, whom Twain described as the South's finest literary genius, escorted the visitors through the Vieux Carré. "With Mr. Cable along to see for you," Twain wrote in *Life on the Mississippi*, "and describe and explain and illuminate, a jog through the old quarter is a vivid pleasure." Howells, who had planned to join the party because Cable's accounts of the city had excited in him a wish to see it, went to Europe instead, but Joel Chandler Harris came over from Atlanta. The children who flocked to get a glimpse of "Uncle Remus" were disappointed to find not only that he was white but that he was indisposed to read to them from his stories. Twain and Cable read the stories for him, "to show him," Twain said, "what an easy trick it was; but his immortal shyness was proof against even this sagacious strategy." They read for the audience, enlarged by the arrival of other guests, from their own works too. "Mr. Cable," Twain said, "is the only master in the writing of French dialects that the country has produced; and he reads them to perfection. It was a great treat to hear him read about Jean-ah Poquelin, and about Innerarity [of *The Grandissimes*] and his famous 'pigshoo' representing 'Louisihanna Rif-fusing to

Hanter the Union,' along with passages of nicely shaded German
dialect from a novel which is still in manuscript."

IV *An Unfortunate Incident*

The manuscript was a draft of the book finally published as
Dr. Sevier. The first version, entitled *Bread,* had dismayed
Gilder who wrote that, in his opinion, it was the poorest work
Cable had done. He thought Cable had given his mind to
philanthropic and civic work so completely as to lose his sense
of art, and he begged that the major characters be spared some
of the misfortunes visited on them. When Robert Underwood
Johnson underscored the objections of his fellow editor, Cable
added, in the course of many revisions, to the picturesque quality
the editors pointedly called for, and he reduced the didacticism
they found so apparent and so objectionable. What Cable read
to Twain must have been a revision of the early installments,
which his editors found more to their liking than the initial
draft. But even in the final version of the book it was clear that
this was, as Gilder said, a story of intention, and that Cable
had defected from conservative Southern tradition.

Not long after Cable played host to Osgood, Twain, and
Harris, he received a letter from Boyesen asking him to present
New Orleans to a professor from the University of Moscow who
wished to study class and race relations in the city. Although
Boyesen and Cable were no longer cast in the roles of mentor
and novice (Cable having achieved a status comparable to that
of his former sponsor), Boyesen had given high praise to *The
Grandissimes* in his review in *Scribner's Monthly,* had seen
Cable occasionally in New York, and could feel confident of his
friend's willingness to grant the favor. When Professor Waldemir
Kowaledsky arrived in June, Cable took him to the lake for a
swim and there presented him to various acquaintances, calling
particular attention to those he said had served as models for
characters in his fiction.

On Kowaledsky's return to Europe he wrote a detailed account
of his visit with Cable in a Russian journal which had recently
printed a translation of one of Cable's Creole tales. To Cable's
embarrassment, the *Critic* published a condensed version of
Kowaledsky's article on July 20, 1883. The Russian reported

Cable as saying he "composed nothing," merely taking his characters from life by careful observation of the Creoles around him, and admitting, "It is not for nothing that the Creoles—my chosen types—do not like me." Yet the Creoles on the beach, Kowaledsky said, crowded around them to shake hands. In reference to the literary discussion in which he and Cable had engaged, Kowaledsky quoted Cable as saying that Boyesen was not an artist but a learned man—one deficient in creative imagination and owning a talent inferior to that of Howells. Cable tried to repair the damage done by his indiscretion. In a characteristically adroit letter which the *Critic* published on August 25, he did not deny the remarks attributed to him but disclaimed any recollection of having made them. He praised Boyesen unreservedly without mentioning Boyesen's direct aid in getting his first books in print, and he cleverly avoided making any comparison of Boyesen and Howells.[7]

The unfortunate incident surely had an adverse effect on a relationship from which Cable had derived great benefit but which was no longer vital to his success. Boyesen had been replaced by more influential patrons. He returned a polite, chilly note of thanks for the copy of *Dr. Sevier* Cable sent as a Christmas present in 1884. But in March, 1895, when other critics were evidencing little enthusiasm for Cable's *John March, Southerner*, Boyesen's generous review in *Cosmopolitan* staunchly defended the controversial novel, which seemed to him to have the same kind of merit he had detected in the prospectus for *The Grandissimes*.

V *Public Readings*

Cable's trip to the North in September, 1882, another step in his conquest of the glittering world of the literati and in the development of a new and more cosmopolitan personal character, led to a solution of his financial problems by introducing him to the possibility of supplementing his income by giving public readings from his works. It differed from earlier visits in that its avowed purpose was to let him work on *Dr. Sevier*. He found he could write in his room on West 22nd Street in New York at a rate impossible in the climate of New Orleans, and his free time could be spent in such a way as to contribute to his professional prospects.

Cable enjoyed the company of Pennell, Waring, Osgood, the Gilders and of such new acquaintances as Brander Matthews, Mary Mapes Dodge, John Burroughs, and George Parsons Lathrop. He converted celebrities right and left, but in one case he was the convert: Joseph Jefferson, renowned for his portrayal of Rip Van Winkle, proved to be as fine a gentleman as he was an actor. Cable's puritanical family tradition and the strict conventions to which his mother-in-law subscribed denounced all stage presentations as sinful. Although this attitude toward the theater was not exceptional at the time, it was not held in the social and literary circles in which Cable now felt at home. (Howells asked Charles Dudley Warner in 1877, "Do nice people go to the theatre in Hartford?" He learned that they did, accepting the drama as a respectable amusement.)[8]

Cable applied his logical mind to the traditional arguments about the moral probity of the theater but delayed revising his first opinion. Finally he attended a play in company with Roswell Smith, of whose piety he stood in no doubt; and a year after his first meeting with Jefferson he went to see him in *The Cricket on the Hearth*. Cable's answer to the "great moral question," he wrote his wife on October 27, 1883, was that the theater was not inherently wrong. It was a relief to find that reason was on the side of his inclination, for Cable had always enjoyed music, and he had a strong dramatic sense. He was prone to perform—to act—both in public and private. Few of his friends were aware of this, and he may not have realized, either, how often he was playing a role rather than being himself.

Cable's whole career would have been adversely affected had he felt obliged to regard the performing arts as sinful. Among his greatest pleasures in New York in 1882 were the evenings with Clara Louise Kellogg, the operatic soprano, who shared his love for Negro and Creole melodies. They took turns in singing these folk tunes for their distinguished friends. These performances, and his acceptance of the propriety of attending the theater, anticipated later developments in his public career.

A welcome solution to his most pressing financial problems and a beginning of his public appearances as a lecturer and platform reader was the arrangement, made through Gilder's intervention, for Cable to deliver a series of lectures at Johns Hopkins University in Baltimore. The income, about $1,000, was badly needed, for only by obtaining monthly advances on *Dr. Sevier* was Cable able to manage the visit to New York. He owed interest on several loans, taxes, and other debts. When he sent $250 to New Orleans, however, he directed that $150 be paid on his subscription to the church debt and that part of what was left be applied to the rent on the house in which his mother, sisters, and the Cox children lived. A devoted worker for the Prytania Street Presbyterian Church, Cable gave generously of time and energy as well as money. His contribution to the church debt was an instance of the kind of strained philanthropy and precarious financial management that disturbed his wife but caused him little concern.

Mark Twain, writing to Howells about the short visit Cable made to Hartford at this time, said: "Cable has been here, creating worshipers on all hands. He is a marvelous talker on a deep subject. . . . You know when it comes down to moral honesty, limpid innocence, and utterly blemishless piety, the Apostles were mere policemen to Cable."[9] Cable's personality, added to his literary reputation and Gilder's efforts on his behalf, surely helped to bring about the Hopkins lecture series. The general topic was "The Relations of Literature to Modern Society," but Cable broke this unwieldy subject into somewhat more reasonable subtitles. He practiced his platform delivery in giving his annual secretary's report to the Prisons and Asylums Aid Association in New Orleans in January, 1883, for he knew he had to make his high, thin voice audible to large audiences.

The Hopkins lectures were scheduled for March 5 through March 16. Cable's friends, who were convinced that he could not support himself without an income other than that derived from his writing, regarded the series as a test of his prospects on the lecture platform. They were relieved by reports from the press and by strong, perhaps exaggerated, statements from Cable testifying to his success in making himself heard.[10] Baltimore critics praised his lectures as comparable to those delivered earlier by Lowell and Sidney Lanier, and Cable was invited to add a final lecture when the series was officially ended. This time he gave readings from his works, enlivened by asides that were not altogether untheatrical.

The evening was such a triumph that a change was made in the plans for his appearance on the platform in Hartford, where

Roswell Smith, Mark Twain, Charles Dudley Warner, and other friends had intended to sponsor a lecture at Unity Hall. At Cable's suggestion, it was decided to substitute readings from his works for the talk he had planned on "Creole Women." The program won such a gratifying response that other readings were given to smaller groups the next day. Cable was jubilant over the applause, the favorable press notices, and the prospect of an important supplement to his income. He wrote his mother that a new future was opening up for him. Because that future depended on learning to use his weak voice effectively, he began voice training and for years he studied and practiced to perfect an art for which he was physically ill-equipped. Master it he did. For many years his platform readings were his financial mainstay, carrying him thousands of miles annually and pushing his writing into almost as secondary a position as it had occupied when he was a counting room clerk.

In June, 1883, when Cable spoke in New Orleans at the commencement of the University of Louisiana (now Tulane University), he was perhaps as much interested in the delivery of his remarks as in their content, for his address on literature was conventional. A year earlier, his speech at the University of Mississippi commencement on "Literature in the Southern States" had sharply criticized the South's devotion to caste, its defense of an institution—slavery—that was a "crime against heaven and humanity," and its pride in being "a unique people" isolated from the world's best thought and literature.[11] Cable had himself in mind when he told his New Orleans audience, somewhat cautiously, that writers must be free to try to rectify the manners and morals of society. Though he did not identify the local reform in which he was most interested at this time, his audience knew he was the spearhead of the movement to improve the city's medieval prisons and asylums. His preoccupation with this civic endeavor had led him to make the first draft of *Dr. Sevier* a tract that, contrary to the principles he had endorsed in his letters to Boyesen, smelled of its moral as small houses do of the meal being cooked in the kitchen. When he finished the book in New York that fall, he did not extract all evidence of his growing disapproval of Southern doctrines and practices, but he made it "picturesque" enough to suit the editors whose demands he was in no position to resist.

CHAPTER 5

The Twain–Cable Menagerie

I Dr. Sevier

CABLE'S second novel, *Dr. Sevier*, began its serial run in *Century Magazine* in November, 1883, and appeared in book form the next year. The New Orleans of *Dr. Sevier* is the city Cable knew as a youth. The opening passages describe the American business district, not the Vieux Carré; the major characters are not Creoles or quadroons. In his third novel, *John March, Southerner*, which does not have a Louisiana setting and includes no Creoles or quadroons, Cable carried his study of Southern problems from 1864 into the 1880's. When he resumed his analysis of Southern society in serious fiction at the very close of his career, he treated the New Orleans of World War I. Yet critics persist in pigeonholing Cable as a local color artist whose subject was ante-bellum Creole New Orleans and its environs. This is much like saying, in summary, that Mark Twain wrote about jumping frogs.

In *The Grandissimes*, Cable noted that Frowenfeld did not become "that complete proselyte that alone satisfies a Creole," and near the end of the book the author made a point of disagreeing with those who believe one should "confine one's patriotic affection to a small fraction of a great country." Much of *Dr. Sevier* was written when Cable was away from his Southern home; and, before the first installments were in circulation, he had begun to appear as a lecturer and reader on widely scattered platforms. He thought he was expressing in this novel the sort of large loyalty the nation was endeavoring to foster and that, by carefully avoiding discussion of the issues that had brought on the Civil War, he might help to heal sectional wounds. In treating with judicial respect the motives and sacrifices of both sides in the struggle, he included sentimental,

Whitmanesque passages praising alike the Union and Confederate heroism of twenty years earlier. But Cable forgot his own analysis of Creole character, forgot that he had used Creoles as symbols for the whole South. He lost the tolerance of his neighbors when he proved he was not the complete proselyte the sensitive South required its citizens to be.

The action of *Dr. Sevier* begins in 1856 and concludes after the fall of New Orleans to Union forces. Dr. Sevier (who is not a Creole)[1] befriends John and Mary Richling, strangers to the city, because he admires their character and is struck by Mary's resemblance to his dead wife. Obviously a "gentleman" unequipped to earn a living, John Richling has no letters of reference because he has never worked and is living under an assumed name. He finds no steady employment. Too proud to admit poverty or ask for help, he and his wife are debilitated by sickness, manual labor, and starvation. When Mary becomes pregnant, Dr. Sevier provides the means for her return to her mother in Milwaukee. John finds work as bookkeeper for a German baker and becomes virtually manager of the business, but for various reasons Mary and her baby daughter remain in the North. It is there, after the war breaks out, that word reaches her of her husband's serious illness. She and the little girl make an epic journey through the battle lines to arrive at the bedside of the dying man, who has just explained to Dr. Sevier the mystery of his identity. Richling points to "simple sectional prejudice" as the villain when he discloses that his wealthy Kentucky family disowned and disinherited him because he married a Northern girl. Dr. Sevier assumes the support of his friend's widow and child and makes Mary the agent of the philanthropies he undertakes in John's memory.

It has been said that Cable was incapable of creating a villain; actually, he was far better at drawing villains than heroes. Dr. Sevier's lack of participation in the main action prevents him from becoming the protagonist the book needs so badly. John Richling may be pitied but not admired; he talks nobly but it is his wife who acts nobly. The misfortunes, which beset the young couple as regularly as they would characters in a radio soap opera, are clearly manipulated to make the Richlings instruments in Cable's campaign for civic—not sectional—reform. At different times Mary and John are patients at the Charity

Hospital, an institution for which Cable felt much the same aversion he had for the Parish Prison, a New Orleans Newgate where John spends a brief confinement that ruins his health. In several strong Dickensian scenes, Cable dramatizes the institutional inadequacies and vices he was working to correct through the Prisons and Asylums Aid Association. His efforts to make the novel a powerful social study were frustrated because his editors regarded any treatment of an inherently unpleasant subject as a tract. Had Gilder's squeamishness not prevented, Cable would have had a villain for his novel: society.

What was left after the specific attacks on social evils were eliminated was little more than the sentimental main plot, a true story Cable was told by Dr. D. Warren Brickell, the model for Dr. Sevier, and one Cable thought had literary merit because his father-in-law wept on hearing it. The novel can be described as social realism only because of Cable's fine presentation of scenes he had observed at first hand and the variety and vitality of his minor characters.

These characters include, perhaps as a kind of trademark, an admirable quadroon nurse and an amusing young Creole. Madame Zenobia is a middle-aged colored woman in whose house the Richlings rent quarters on first coming to New Orleans. She nurses both young people in their serious illnesses and becomes Mary's companion when John dies. Creoles, who had blushed with shame or flushed with anger over such figures as Jules St.-Ange of "Posson Jone'" and Raoul Innerarity of *The Grandissimes*, could take no pleasure in Narcisse, who keeps the office of Dr. Sevier. The handsome scamp is an inveterate borrower who has no scruples about taking from the Richlings the last dollar that stands between them and starvation. They cannot resist his pleas and promises, though they know him for the sham he is. His Byronic pose and ridiculous speech provide moments of comedy sorely needed to relieve the prevailing mood of misery.

"Mistoo Itchlin . . . do you not fine me impooving in my p'onouncement of yo' lang-widge? I fine I don't use such bad land-widge [sic] like biffo. I am shue you muz' 'ave notiz since some time I soun' that awer in you' name. Mistoo Itchlin, will you 'ave that kin'ness to baw me two-an-a-'alf till the lass of that month?"

An excellent yellow fever nurse, Narcisse makes his services available only on a cash basis—ten dollars a night in advance. Cable does not supply a more commendable Creole as foil for Narcisse, and he makes Narcisse too ignoble to be redeemed by the announcement of his death in battle as a Confederate hero. Gilder, always attracted by the picturesque, thought Dr. Sevier's office boy one of the best of Cable's creations. Creoles had little reason to agree with Gilder or to contribute to the praise readers in England and America showered on the novel.

Filling out the range of character types and contributing new possibilities for dialect are Irish Kate Riley, Italian Raphael Ristofalo, a Mississippi backwoodsman named Sam, and the Reisens, a German baker and his wife. These are all excellent characters, but Cable renders their speech with a sometimes tediously conscientious accuracy. He seems to handle best the Irish brogue, which he used frequently in later work, though he is guilty of employing false dialect when he has Kate Riley speak grandly of her second husband's acquaintance with "Garrybaldy." The lengths to which Cable went in experimenting with orthography and speech peculiarities may be seen in his representation of a lisping rector, a man genuinely interested in charity, whose friends laugh at his concern about whether "aththithtanth aththithtth."

From the several chapters describing Mary's journey to her husband's bedside, the best chapters in the book, Cable extracted a selection that became his stand-by on the reading platform. Gradually he extended its length from six minutes to about fifteen.[2] It is hard to say whether his colleague, Mark Twain, found "Mary's Night Ride" annoying because he thought it sentimental drivel or because it was a favorite with their audiences. Aware of the humorous and demeaning effects dialect may produce, Cable used it sparingly in the dialogue of the Union spy, the Mississippi backwoodsman who guides Mary through the lines. Sam has Cable's full approval, so there is none of the arch delicacy, sly condescension, or lofty moralizing that mars the delineation of many of his characters. Neither improved nor debased by his creator, the backwoodsman has an honest vitality that Joel Chandler Harris recognized as impressive.

Cable's character and changing fortunes are clearly reflected in *Dr. Sevier.* First, his exposure to Northern attitudes shows in his wish to expand his subject matter, to make it representative of the nation rather than of one section alone. Secondly, the attack on New Orleans hospitals and prisons manifests his quickening interest in civic reform. Thirdly, his pious moralizing and his confidence in his abilities as a lay prophet are apparent in the Bible interpretations he assigns to Richling and Dr. Sevier. Fourthly, the physician's conversion to philanthropy and Mary's commitment to a life of social service foretell the direction Cable's own career was to take.

The novel also provides an insight into some of the author's less attractive qualities. Long a bookkeeper but now a professional writer, Cable suggests that accounting is not a suitable occupation for a gentleman. So deferential to people he thought his superiors that he seemed almost to fawn on them, Cable could only patronize anyone he considered his inferior. Like most Americans at that time, he did not regard the varied national types he depicted as his equals. First-generation immigrants might deserve respect and should be helped to find their proper place in society, but necessary social lines must be preserved. Cable, for example, seems amused at Reisen's satisfaction in being called "Mr.," a title Dr. Sevier carefully refrains from bestowing on him, and "lady" is put in quotation marks when applied to Kate Riley. In describing the wedding of Kate and Raphael Ristofalo, Richling reports to Dr. Sevier the "broad Hibernian repartee" he heard there and mimics "the brogue of two or three Irish gentlemen, and the soft, outlandish swing in the English of one or two Sicilians." Richling and Dr. Sevier, both spokesmen for Cable, find the wedding droll though they have every reason to esteem the bride and groom. A resourceful, courageous man, Ristofalo is neither censured nor ridiculed, perhaps because he has the gift of making money. This seemed no small talent to Cable, who admired rich men and exulted in the evidences of wealth he saw on his visits to Broadway.

But Cable's picture of an incident on Broadway, June 1, 1861, was his undoing in *Dr. Sevier*. Mary Richling, who has missed the last steamer for New Orleans, stands there to watch a parade of Union soldiers, a scene much like that Thomas Nast painted of New York's Seventh Regiment marching down Broadway on April 19, 1861. Cable closes his description with a lyric passage: " 'go marching on,' saviors of the Union; your cause is just. Lo, now, since nigh twenty-five years have passed, we of the South can say it!" Despite his efforts to evade entanglement in the issues of the war and to refrain from any show of partisanship, there are hints that Cable's affectionate memories of his Confederate comrades were outweighed by his aversion to slavery and secession. His portrait of the soldiers and non-combatants whom Mary encounters on her way through the lines is superbly realistic, entirely free of stylized pictures of Northern villainy and Southern nobility. He took no advantage of the opportunity to dramatize the fall of New Orleans, which he had witnessed as a youth, or to show the proud city humbled by the highhanded rule of General "Beast" Butler. The Richlings are Union sympathizers, and Dr. Sevier's support of the Confederacy is late and reluctant. Cable did not need to say directly in the novel that he thought justice was on the side of the North. He had already made his position clear.

II *Departure from the South*

The last chapters of *Dr. Sevier* were finished just before the first installment was published. The writing was done as part of a pleasant routine, for Cable had time to spend with Gilder, Roswell Smith, and Joseph Jefferson and opportunities to meet such celebrities as Andrew Carnegie, Matthew Arnold, and Saint-Gaudens. His need to juggle his debts was relieved by appearances as a platform reader. At Boston's Chickering Hall he won real acclaim, with Howells and Oliver Wendell Holmes adding their praise to that of the newspapers. Edward Everett Hale offered to be his host; and Whittier, who called at his hotel room, said he had read every line Cable had written and knew from his first productions that he would attain greatness. In December, Cable wrote home that he was the fashion of the day, that success was pouring in on him like a flood. After spending the Christmas holidays in New Orleans, he made a platform tour under the management of Major James B. Pond, and on January 21, 1884, he read for the first time in Northampton, Massachusetts, which was later to be his home.

In February, *Century Magazine* published Cable's essay, "The Convict Lease System in the Southern States," a detailed analysis of the practice of leasing prisoners as laborers to the highest bidder. Crowded with facts and figures, the essay was the product of prolonged research and showed Cable to be an objective scholar, a persuasive social critic, and a practical humanitarian. He pointed out that it was no more logical to expect prisoners to pay for their incarceration than to demand that schools, courts, legislatures, and police departments be self-supporting. Prisoners were treated with such extreme brutality that few survived a sentence of more than ten years. Cable proved that Louisiana's guilt was particularly heavy and that the system as it operated in all the Southern states was a disgrace that called for immediate correction. Of course the article was a parallel to the attack on New Orleans prisons woven into *Dr. Sevier*. To Southerners it seemed to border on treason to his heritage.

The strength of that heritage was steadily diminishing and, notwithstanding public protestations to the contrary, Cable felt less and less a Southerner. His stay at Mark Twain's home in the winter, unexpectedly prolonged when he came down with the mumps, was followed by a successful season of readings that helped to modify his sectional perspective. In April he wrote his wife: "The South makes me sick, the West makes me tired, the East makes me glad. It is the intellectual treasury of the United States. Here is cultivation, & refinement, & taste."[3]

This preference was strengthened by events of the next few months. In May, when he gave in New Orleans the same kind of reading program that had won enthusiastic applause elsewhere, the presence of a large audience was comforting evidence of Southern recognition of his achievement as author and reader. But when he spoke on the position of the Negro in the contemporary South at the University of Alabama in June, his remarks were received for the first time without any commendation. Alabama papers joined the Creoles in condemning him, and even the New Orleans press, generally friendly, regarded the address as unfortunate. The number of his detractors mounted steadily.

It must have been with great relief that Cable moved his family to Connecticut in July, a step that signaled his permanent departure from the South. Friends had arranged for them to rent a house in Simsbury, Connecticut, for a year of temporary residence. One motive for the change of address was to escape the dangers and debilitating effects of New Orleans' humid, plague-ridden summers. Another, Cable said, was to put him closer to his publishers and the audiences for his readings. Certainly a third was that by this time he found the region to which he was moving a more congenial and financially rewarding place to live than his native South. Ever since he first thought of making literature his profession he had wished for the stimulating association with other writers and artists and the cultural benefits to be gained by living in or near the major financial and intellectual centers of the nation. No doubt he leased his Eighth Street home, which was occupied for a time by Joaquin Miller, less with a sense of retreating before his neighbors' hostility—not yet fully aroused—than of advancing toward a more enriching experience.

III   *Twain and Cable*

A more important document than the lease was the contract Cable signed with Mark Twain in mid-July. For several years Twain had thought of sponsoring a reading tour—"a menagerie"—to include Cable, Howells, Joel Chandler Harris, Thomas Bailey Aldrich, and himself. The final arrangement, however, included only Twain and Cable. Twain took all the risks, hired Cable at $450 a week plus expenses for twenty weeks, and engaged Major Pond as traveling manager. The two performers—"Twins of Genius" Pond called them—shared equal billing when they took to the road in November.

The installment of *Dr. Sevier* in which Cable conceded the justice of the Union cause had brought vigorous opposition, to which he responded in defense of his conciliatory lines in an open letter in the November issue of *Century Magazine*. Since it asserted his "complete conviction" that the Union's cause was just, the statement did not restore him to favor or win him authorization to say again "we of the South." It was his defection from Southern principles, not his move from New Orleans, that denied him the right to speak *for* his native region. For a few more years he was able to speak occasionally in the South on the problems he studied so carefully and, after platforms there were closed to him, to direct his printed opinions to Southern audiences. But he learned that Southerners would accept criticism from him no more readily than they would from a Northerner; that any deviation from the accepted sectional doctrines made him a renegade. The tour with Twain, which took the readers to eighty-five cities, helped to strengthen Cable's political liberalism. Whatever incompatibilities disturbed the relationship of the two men, they held very similar views about slavery, the nation's obligation to the freedmen, and the right of every Negro to be treated according to his individual merit.

Both were the children of slaveholders, but Twain's father had recognized the injustice of the institution. As early as 1882, Howells said that Twain in his character had none of the narrowness of the Missouri community in which he was reared; "it does not appear in his books, where there is not an ungenerous line, but always, on the contrary, a burning resentment of all manner of cruelty and wrong."[4] A Union sympathizer, Twain had been a Confederate soldier for a few days, and his contribution to the *Century Magazine* series on Battles and Leaders of the Civil War,[5] for which Cable wrote "New Orleans Before the Capture," was "The Private History of a Campaign that Failed," an account of mock soldiering altogether unlike Cable's strenuous tour of duty. Both men had known colored people as slaves and servants and both came to know and respect some of the leaders of the freedmen, but Twain's relationship with Negroes showed an acceptance of them as people and, in some instances, a personal affection that Cable did not match. It was regard for individual Negroes he had known that led Twain to create the magnificent figure of Jim in *The Adventures of Huckleberry Finn*, the "hymn to brotherhood"[6] published while he was on tour with Cable. But Twain was guided by principle as much as by emotion. When he paid the expenses of a Negro student at Yale, an act he performed anonymously for a man he did not know, he did so, according to Howells, in partial fulfillment of what he thought was the obligation of very white man to every freedman. Shortly before his readings with Cable began, Twain wrote Howells of how his rage had disappeared when he learned that the author of an unpolished letter he had resented was a Negro minister, whose ignorance might be excused. He told Howells his wife had said a "bright thing" in suggesting a motto to guide his future conduct: "Consider every man colored till he is proved white."[7]

Huckleberry Finn affords ample evidence that Twain and Cable were in accord in their position on the nation's race controversy. "Good gracious!" Aunt Polly says when Huck tells her of an accident on a river boat, "anybody hurt?" Relieved to learn that the only victim is "a nigger," she says: "Well, it's lucky, because sometimes people do get hurt." In satire the dullest reader could not misinterpret, Twain depicts an encounter between a Negro of brains and breeding and a white man lacking in both. Drunken Pap Finn, who regards his son's ability to read and write as putting on airs—"None of the family couldn't before *they* died!"—reports meeting at Judge Thatcher's home a visiting free Negro from Ohio who was "most as white as a white man." The Negro wears "fine clothes"; Pap is in rags.

> They said he was p'fessor in a college, and could talk all kinds of languages, and knowed everthing. And that ain't the wust. They said he could *vote* when he was at home. Well, that let me out. Thinks I, what is the country a-coming to? It was 'lection day, and I was just about to go and vote myself if I waren't too drunk to get there; but when they told me there ,was a state in this country where they'd let that nigger vote, I drawed out. . . . And to see the cool way of that nigger—why, he wouldn't 'a' give me the road if I hadn't shoved him out o' the way.[8]

Twain wrote of an even fairer Negro in *Puddinhead Wilson* (1894), a novel to which some modern critics have assigned virtues that are entirely the product of their own imaginations. This tale of two infants, one white and the other the child of an octoroon slave, who are exchanged (a twist on the mistaken identity plot Twain had used earlier in *The Prince and the Pauper*), leaves obscure the author's opinions about inherited racial traits. (Cable's *John March, Southerner,* published at about the same time, has a similar ambiguity.) Twain's readers may suppose he agrees with his character's statement that the slightest trace of Negro blood in a man is enough to "paint his soul." Howells, who wrote of miscegenation in a short novel, *An Imperative Duty* (1891), in which the heroine discovers that she is the daughter of a New Orleans octoroon whose father was a Creole, said in *My Mark Twain* that his friend scorned the shabby philosophy that a man who was fifteen parts white would be debased by the fraction of blood that branded him a Negro.

But if Twain and Cable were in agreement on the race question, they were an ill-matched pair in other respects. Twain's rangy figure towered over that of his small companion. His heavy mustache was like a brush, while Cable's drooped at the ends almost to the tip of his pointed beard. They often capitalized on the physical contrasts by walking on stage together, or Cable might appear alone and introduce himself by saying, "I'm not Mark Twain." Twain's readings provoked the roars of laughter, Cable's the lighter laughs and tears; he wrote home with pride about the woman who cried throughout "Mary's Night Ride." Twain adopted the straight-faced delivery of the Western narrator of tall tales, drawling his stories with a twang, seeming to extemporize, as he slouched against the lectern. His selections, changed more often from night to night than Cable's, frequently included "The Jumping Frog from Calaveras County" and episodes from *Huckleberry Finn*. Cable's manner was more animated; his steps were quick; his hazel eyes twinkled. Most of his readings were from *Dr. Sevier*, just published as a book, and often he sang Creole and Rebel songs in his high nasal voice. Twain was volatile, unpredictable, easily roused to a wrath he was likely to regret. Swearing was for him an art he relished, but Cable never said anything stronger than "plague on it."[9]

They were diametrically opposed in regard to religion. Twain, who did not acknowledge the divinity of Jesus, was irritated by Cable's puritanical piety and inclined to regard it as religiosity. Cable's Sabbatarianism, particularly his refusal to travel on Sunday, was a great inconvenience to the touring party. In letters to his wife Twain sometimes protested bitterly about what he considered to be parsimony on Cable's part; he did not take into proper account Cable's heavy responsibilities and precarious financial predicament. Twain was, however, on more defensible ground in objecting to Cable's petty dishonesty in announcing a new program when he merely repeated the selections he had read the previous night. The criticisms may be dismissed, generally, as expressions of Twain's emotional instability enhanced by the strain of the long train rides, the readings in basements and churches, and the pressures of continuous public appearances. The outbursts were not unprovoked, but they were probably inflated to unjustified proportions in the letters he sent home. Cable's letters to his wife convey their message by innuendo and, when read with an understanding of his character, seem evidences of what Twain called his "colossal self-conceit,"[10] a vanity that drove him to indirect slurs and slyly ungenerous comments on Twain's abilities. Mark Twain's letters are spontaneous; Cable's seem snide and calculating. Neither man had reason to disparage the other's platform performance, for each was a superb reader. Audience reaction and press notices varied in the different cities, but the readings were widely acclaimed and both men highly praised. The tour was a memorable experience. For Cable, coming though it did near the beginning of his long career on the reading platforms of the nation, it was a climax unequaled in the rest of his life.

One especially fortunate occurrence in January was Cable's recommendation of *Morte d'Arthur*, which Twain had not read. Twain was taken by Malory's quaint language, and he and Cable made a game of using it to each other. Soon an entry on the inconveniences of metal clothing appeared in Twain's notebook, and a few years later his interest culminated in *A Connecticut Yankee in King Arthur's Court*. Cable said Twain called him the godfather of that book. If the outrage against which the novel is directed is "not Arthurian but Southern slavery,"[11] Cable's part in it was more than that of introducing Twain to Malory. The controversy in which Cable was embroiled at this time kept slavery very much in the minds of the twins of genius.

CHAPTER 6

From Sahara to Paradise

I *Liberal Racial Views*

HOWELLS' *The Rise of Silas Lapham* and a selection from Twain's *Huckleberry Finn* were in the *Century Magazine* for January, 1885, in which Cable's "The Freedman's Case in Equity" appeared. That essay, a revised version of his remarks at the University of Alabama commencement and at a meeting of the American Social Science Association in Saratoga, New York, was inspired by an episode Cable had witnessed on a train ride to Louisville, Kentucky. He saw a well-dressed, refined colored woman and her small daughter forced to ride in a car with a band of filthy convicts, an indignity and discomfort the woman would not have had to suffer—however loathsome she might have been—had the girl been white and she the child's hired guardian. On a train bearing Cable and Twain away from Louisville in January, 1885, Twain observed a similar incident. He was infuriated by a country boy's loud, insulting remarks about a colored passenger in the car, a woman, Twain wrote to his wife, who was better dressed and had more brains and breeding than several generations of the white boy's family could show. Cable's essay was an incisive analysis of the position of the Negro in America that urged that the freedman be granted the civil rights to which all citizens were entitled. With this article Cable assumed the unpopular role of champion of the Negro; his name became anathema in the South and the subject of controversy across the country.

His gradual conversion to liberal racial views resulted from thoughtful reading, research into Louisiana history, exposure to Northern influences, strong humanitarian inclinations, and the application of an objective and inexorable logic to a topic few of his associates could consider unemotionally. Reared as a Southerner, a member of a slaveholding family, and a resident of a particularly caste-conscious community, Cable grew up as a typical supporter of the doctrine of the inequality of men. When war came he cheered the stars and bars and risked his life in battle for the Confederate cause. His disillusionment began after the war with doubts about the wisdom of secession as a political principle. He heard it said that the Civil War settled that political controversy, but he could not see how force could resolve an issue based on principle. With the doctrine of secession abandoned, the justice of the Southern cause hinged on the righteousness of slavery as an institution, and men said that question, too, had been answered on the battlefield. If secession and slavery were indefensible, then the subjugation of one people by another, whatever name it might be given, was also wrong. Any government designed to preserve a caste system —to deny men the enjoyment of public rights on the basis of their birth—was a poor government and the agent of an unjust social order. Cable concluded that the perpetuation of the freedman's fixed and inferior status through segregation and the denial of civil rights degraded the Negro and corrupted the white man who exploited him.

The course of action on which Cable was now embarked was exactly that which his spokesman, Frowenfeld, had urged on the quadroon Honoré Grandissime.

> I can imagine a man in your place, going about among his people, stirring up their minds to a noble discontent, laying out his means, sparingly here and bountifully there, as in each case might seem wisest, for their enlightenment, their moral elevation, their training in skilled work; going, too, among the people of the prouder caste, among such as have a spirit of fairness, and seeking to prevail with them for a public recognition of the rights of all; using all his cunning to show them the double damage of all oppression, both great and petty—

But Cable made himself heir to the cause of William Lloyd Garrison, Wendell Phillips, and the others he called "the great dead"[1] at a time when that cause seemed lost. Tired of the dispute that had plunged the nation into war, the North wished to see the sections reconciled, and to this end it conceded to the

South the right to solve the race problem as it saw fit. As Albion Tourgée pointed out in *A Fool's Errand* (1879) and *Bricks Without Straw* (1880), this doomed the Negro to a servile status. When the Supreme Court invalidated the civil rights statutes in 1883, returning to the states the determination of the civil status of the freedmen, the Democratic Solid South won a victory Confederate troops had been denied.

This victory was apparent in the national literature, which painted the ante-bellum plantation with romantic color and depicted the Negro as undeserving of the rights of citizenship. It was evident in the pages of *Century Magazine*. In the February issue, in which *The Bostonians* of Henry James began its serial run, the editors rebuked deprecating, bitter partisanship by Northerners, a move intended to forestall any charge that the journal had printed Cable's article in that spirit. In March an editorial note remarked on the very large number of letters Cable's essay had provoked, only a few of them "reminders of the good old-fashioned bowie-knife and fire-eating days." The letters flooded in on Cable while he was on the reading tour, and Mark Twain, who did not become embroiled in the race controversy, gave his friend "points" to be used in answering the Louisiana and Georgia Bourbons.

A Georgian, Henry W. Grady,[2] was commissioned by *Century* to reply to Cable. His "In Plain Black and White" was published in April and was followed on the next pages by Cable's "New Orleans Before the Capture." Cable's rejoinder to Grady, "The Silent South," did not appear until September. Two months later, this article, "The Freedman's Case in Equity," and "The Convict Lease System in the Southern States" were issued as *The Silent South*.

Cable had become a sort of post-bellum abolitionist. When he spoke for Negro rights on the lecture platform and when he turned his "grey goose quill" into the crusader's lance and assaulted the wall of discrimination and disfranchisement the New South had erected, bitter indignation swept the South. It was not Creoles alone who spat at mention of his name, for his subject was not miscegenation in old Louisiana or the horrors of the Black Code; it was the violation of the ideals of Jeffersonian democracy in the flagrant mistreatment of millions of American citizens being victimized because of their race. In

Dr. Sevier his praise of the blue-clad "saviors of the Union" seemed a repudiation of all that the Confederacy had stood for. The decade that followed, the heroic period of Cable's life, saw him challenge virtually all the premises on which his former neighbors were building the New South.

II *Northampton and Social Acceptance*

Criticism in the press of "The Freedman's Case in Equity" was so voluminous and so uniformly acrimonious that any thought Cable might have had of returning to the South to live vanished. He wrote his wife in Simsbury on January 31, 1885: "I must admit that I shall not from choice bring up my daughters in that state of society. The more carefully I study it the less I expect of it; and though there is no reason why I should indulge ungracious feelings toward it I cannot admire it or want my children to be brought up under its influence."[3] When he visited New Orleans briefly in March, he discovered that even some of his closest friends found his presence a trial.

Soon after he returned to Connecticut, he was troubled by widespread newspaper abuse and reports that the tour with Twain had broken up in a row. Most of the slanders were directed against Cable, who wrote vigorous public denials. Pond said nothing and advised him to ignore the matter as trivial. With this advice the usually explosive Twain surprisingly concurred, perhaps because he had inadvertently sparked the newspaper stories; it was ten years before Twain publicly denied that there had been a quarrel. The controversy was still current in the press when William Cable was born. With the birth of his sixth child, the first to arrive in the North, Cable could no longer call his home "The House of Seven Cables" or say of his children that "half of them are girls and the other half are girls too."[4]

By the time *The Silent South* was issued in November, 1885, the Cables had taken up permanent residence in Northampton, Massachusetts. The decision to live in the North was made for Cable, rather than by him; he was no longer welcome in New Orleans. He had been advised that the notes he still owed on his Eighth Street home would not be renewed, and a court appraiser had assessed the property at an outrageously unjust figure. In any case, his choice of a home in the midst of a social system and culture he approved, and near his publishers and the audience for his readings was a reasonable one. Some critics have found in his flight from New Orleans an explanation for what they regard as a loss of literary power, attributing that loss to his removal from the scenes of his writing. The convenient explanation is a *non sequitur*. The nature and quality of Cable's later work may be traced more properly to a variety of other factors, including in particular the literary taste of the nation and the changes in the author's personal character. In leaving the South, a region increasingly alien to his spirit and hostile to his person but not estranged from his affections, he followed a pattern to which Mark Twain conformed in settling in Hartford and Howells in taking up residence in Belmont, Massachusetts. Bret Harte and Joaquin Miller similarly deserted their native sections for the greater cultural and economic attractions they found elsewhere. James Lane Allen and Walter Hines Page later found life in the South inconvenient. Unlike Joel Chandler Harris, Cable was not expressing the accepted values of his native region in his writing. He could hardly have remained in New Orleans and continued to write about it. And he could not make a living there as either writer or platform reader.

Cable had been charmed by Northampton—which Jenny Lind had called the "Paradise of America—from the time of his first visit, and its location made a practical appeal. About equally distant from New York and Boston, it provided good railroad connections for the more distant places to which he must expect to travel for reading engagements. Within a few hours' ride were a hundred towns and cities where he might find audiences. And no small attraction to a man concerned about educating a house full of daughters was the presence of Smith College, which granted free tuition to Northampton girls who could meet its requirements.

Sentiment as well as logic would have supported the selection of the little city on the Connecticut River. Just as its location accorded with Cable's needs and ambitions, its history and character met his ideals. There was a host of notable native sons and residents who were a source of pride not so much for their business and professional achievements as for their civic services and public benefactions. Jonathan Edwards preached in Northampton from 1727 to 1750. Caleb Strong, one of its most famous sons and eleven times governor of Massachusetts, was a conservative whose career made the Northampton area a stronghold for political, religious, and social orthodoxy; but there was also a contrary tradition in the region. Shays' Rebellion took place in Hampshire County, and the town of Florence, three miles from Northampton, was long a center for various kinds of radical thought.

In the early 1840's Florence was the home of the Northampton Association of Education and Industry, which resembled such other idealistic social experiments established in the state as Hopedale, Brook Farm, and Fruitlands. Members of the community accepted the duty to perform productive labor for the common good, respected freedom of conscience, and granted equal rights to all without regard to sex, race, or religion. Among the speakers who addressed Florence audiences were Ralph Waldo Emerson, Bronson Alcott, Louisa May Alcott, Julia Ward Howe, Susan B. Anthony, Elizabeth Cady Stanton, William Lloyd Garrison, Wendell Phillips, Theodore Weld, Frederick Douglass, and Robert Ingersoll. Florence was the home of Lydia Maria Child, and Sojourner Truth found a haven there. It was one of the stations of the underground railroad, and nearby Northampton, though more conservative, had its share of antislavery workers. One of these was David Ruggles, a free Negro active in the abolitionist movement, who operated his famous Northampton Water Cure establishment two and a half miles from the center of town in the 1840's. He gave hydropathic treatment to Sojourner Truth, to Garrison, and to doctors, lawyers, clergymen, slaveholders, and abilitionists from all parts of the nation and some foreign countries.

Northampton had a population of only seven thousand in 1862, but it sent 751 men to fight in the Civil War and paid $71,500 in bounties to aid enlistment. Originally a Puritan town, Northampton had only three voters of other than Yankee stock in 1845, but the rise of manufacturing in the next few years brought such an influx of immigrants—Irish, Poles, Germans, French-Canadians, and others—that in 1885 one-third of the thirteen thousand citizens were foreign born. When Cable moved his family into "Red House" on Paradise Road, Northamton had good schools, an opera house, and a sophisticated cultural tradition to which the academic and public programs of Smith College and neighboring Amherst and Mount Holyoke contributed very considerably.

Cable's social acceptance in his new home and the public role he came to fill in the community may be seen in his connection with the Northampton Social and Literary Club, to which he was elected in September, 1885. The purpose of the organization, founded in 1862, was to encourage the regular exchange of knowledge and opinion among its twelve members, all men, new members being admitted only when there was a vacancy. Invariably a meeting took place after election day in November, when the topic for discussion was always the state of the union. Thereafter meetings were held until late spring, though the prescribed pattern of meeting on alternate Wednesdays was rarely adhered to. There were no officers and each member served in turn as host to the others for dinner, generally at his own home; as secretary; and as speaker or leader of the discussion on a topic of his choice. Cable's first performance as discussion leader came in November, 1886, when he opened the meeting with remarks on "The Southern Question." Among the members, the group was known simply as "The Club," but outsiders often called it the Wednesday Evening Club or the Old Club, to distinguish it from several similar organizations, and sometimes they referred to the distinguished body with playful irreverence as "the twelve apostles." In 1887, when Cable talked on "Fiction as a Vehicle of Truth," the membership included the president of Smith College, five Smith professors, the superintendent of Northampton State Hospital, a Congregational minister, a District Court judge, a lawyer and manufacturer, and a bank president.

The minister was the pastor of Edwards Congregational Church, with which Cable was affiliated for the rest of his life. Since his boyhood in New Orleans, Cable had been an active church worker. He became superintendent of the Mission Sunday School of the Prytania Street Presbyterian Church at about the time of his marriage, and he and his wife devoted themselves to this work, adding training in housekeeping, cleanliness, and sewing to the religious instruction of their pupils, many of whom were immigrants. Cable became a deacon of the church

in 1882, at a time when he was beginning to question some of
the strict Presbyterian tenets. Two years later, when the family
was in Connecticut, Cable taught Sunday School there, perhaps
because of the influence of Roswell Smith. Whenever he was
away from home on Sunday, he attended religious services,
often several on the same day, and he did not confine himself
to Protestant churches or to any one denomination. Once in
Louisville when on his tour with Twain he attended services
at an African-Methodist-Temperance Church. Though he pretended otherwise, he was delighted whenever he was recognized
and asked to teach Sunday School. Soon after he moved to
Northampton he began to teach an adult class, first at Edwards
Church and later in the Opera House, but his interpretations
were "too liberalizing, and such pressure was brought to bear
that he had to cease."[5]

In 1887, he began to conduct a Bible study class on Saturday
afternoons in Boston's Tremont Temple for the Boston Sunday
School Teachers' Union. The satisfaction of instructing a weekly
audience of about two thousand people and the nominal salary
he received for the work proved inadequate compensation for
the inconvenience this Saturday commitment caused, so he resigned in November of the following year. Again there had been
objections to his liberal interpretations of doctrine. Cable's non-
sectarian approach to Bible study may be seen in the short
articles he wrote for the *Sunday School Times,* and was evident
in the speech, "Cobwebs in the Church," which he read at
meetings of laymen in 1887.

In June of that year he took on another public responsibility
when he became a trustee of Williston Seminary, probably at
the instigation of A. Lyman Williston, a fellow member of the
Northampton Social and Literary Club. Williston, a descendant
of the founder of the seminary, was treasurer of the board of
trustees of this Easthampton boarding school for boys. The
Samuel Williston who established the school in 1841 was a
prosperous Easthampton button manufacturer and son of the
Reverend Payson Williston. Both the father, who used crutches
for forty years because of a knee injury, and his son were cured
by David Ruggles' hydropathic treatments, which made them
enthusiastic supporters of the Negro "doctor" and his water
cure establishment. Perhaps their gratitude accounts for the fact

that Williston Seminary (now Williston Academy) adopted a liberal racial policy at an early date and admitted occasional Negro students. This would have made a special appeal to Cable, a supporter of several Negro and integrated schools, who remained convinced throughout his life that it was of paramount importance for Negroes and underprivileged whites to have full access to educational institutions. A fairly active trustee, Cable often addressed the students, participated in public programs and ceremonies, and supervised landscape gardening on the campus.[6]

III *Articles and Bonaventure*

The various obligations Cable assumed at this period did little to divert him from his interest in the Southern problem. His assumption of the role of champion of Negro rights, at a time when the position of the colored citizen was at its nadir, could not fail to affect the books and articles he produced between 1884 and 1894, when his commitment to the unpopular and unrewarding campaign came to an end with the serial publication of *John March, Southerner.*

Two of his most interesting pieces, "The Dance in Place Congo" and "Creole Slave Songs," came out in *Century Magazine* in February and April, 1886.[7] In his discussion of the diverse African tribal types and the treatment of slave field hands, Cable demonstrated again the thoroughness of his research into Louisiana history. He spelled out what he had said in his fiction about Creole superstition, the exploitation of the quadroon caste, and the viciousness of the *Code Noir.* In *The Grandissimes,* Frowenfeld is advised not to bother to distinguish one Grandissime from another ("Take them in the mass—as you would shrimp," Dr. Keene says), but underlying Cable's essays on the folk culture of the slaves of Creole Louisiana is an insistence that Negroes must be regarded as individuals who differ in physical appearance, cultural tradition, intellectual capacity, and personal character. He printed the words and music of some of the songs he had collected; the words he worked into some of his fiction, and the songs were part of his platform repertoire. His articles show the importance of preserving and studying these folk materials, which he treats with respect, and they have continuing interest for students of folk culture.

Far from attaining the broad tolerance that let Mark Twain claim for himself no prejudices of color, caste, or creed and, specifically, freedom from any anti-Semitic bias, Cable could write in "Au Large" of "rat-faced Isaacs and Jacobs"; yet it was not the Negro alone whose plight elicited his sympathy. As a member of a surveying party working along the banks of the Atchefalaya River in 1866, Cable became interested in the Acadians. These descendants of Nova Scotian exiles were settled in southwestern Louisiana. A unique minority group, mainly small farmers, they were scorned by Creole planter aristocracy and were unwelcome in New Orleans. Cable visited the Acadian country on several occasions, particularly in connection with his commission for the Tenth Census, and he accumulated detailed notes on their way of life. Although he knew that their oddities of speech and manner constituted their literary attraction in that age of local color, he was admittedly concerned about them as victims of Creole reproach and as symbols for the Southern poor white. He told a St. Louis reporter who interviewed him in January, 1885, when he was touring with Mark Twain, that the Acadians, about whom he hoped to write some day, would be the leaders of Louisiana in the future.

Two years after that interview, the first installment of "Carancro" appeared in *Century Magazine*. That story was followed in March by a second, "Grande Pointe." When "Au Large" finished its five-month run in the magazine a year later, the three stories, sharing a common background and characters, were published as *Bonaventure*. The subtitle, *A Prose Pastoral of Acadian Louisiana*, is an acknowledgment of the romantic emphasis in theme and action. But the stories are more than idylls, for Cable used them as vehicles for mild social criticism.

The one Creole characteristic which Cable found most objectionable, perhaps because of his feelings about his own ancestry, was Creole pride in descent from aristocratic forbears. Acadians he found more appealing:

> . . . in France their race had been peasants; in Acadia, forsaken colonists; in Massachusetts, Pennsylvania, Maryland, Virginia, exiles alien to the land, the language, and the times; in St. Domingo, penniless, sick, unwelcome refugees; and for just one century in Louisiana the jest of the proud Creole, held down by the triple fetter of illiteracy, poverty, and the competition of unpaid, half-clad, swarming slaves.

Cable thought their history all poetry and pathos and their humble origin no dishonor. His spokesman in "Au Large," an energetic American bookseller named George W. Tarbox, remarks that some Creoles are descendants of French nobility, while the Acadians are of peasant stock. But Tarbox, whose hardy exuberance reminds one of Mark Twain's characters, thinks the Acadian's lineage more admirable than the Creole's, a convenient point of view for a man who is the suitor of Madame Zoséphine Beausoleil.

> "—Wouldn't any fair-minded person that knows what France was two or three hundred years ago . . . about as lief be descended from a good deal of that peasantry as from a good deal of that nobility? I should smile! Why . . . the day's coming when the Acadians will be counted as good French blood as there is in Louisiana! They're the only white people that ever trod this continent—island or mainland—who never on their own account oppressed anybody."

Bonaventure, a Creole orphan who grows up among the Acadians, has an unfortunate love affair, recounted in "Carancro," which leads him to dedicate his life to the service of others and thus to personify the theme of the book. (Cable had already made it apparent in the figures of Dr. Sevier and Mary Richling that he thought good works the road to public and personal salvation, and he was very conscious of the nobility of his own benevolence.) Because the main problems of the Acadians are poverty and illiteracy, Bonaventure becomes a school teacher. In the memorable classroom scenes in "Grande Pointe" he struggles earnestly to teach "puffection in the English tongue, whether speaking aw otherwise," and he is "not satisfied whilst the slightest accent of French is remaining." Cable uses Creole and Acadian dialects to provide sentiment and humor, but his picture of Acadian schooling underscores the need, which he discussed later in essays, for Federal aid to education in the South.

In "Carancro," in stating his sympathy for the Acadians conscripted into Confederate service, he again denies that the Southern cause was just. Although *Bonaventure* contains some asides favorable to the Negro, the book maintains its pastoral quality by avoiding controversy and direct partisanship. Education and religion are endorsed, but it is brotherly love that is Bonaventure's doctrine: "Every man not for self, but for every other!" It is the Acadian's potential, what he may become rather than what he is, that wins the author's respect. It is the Acadian—like Claude St. Pierre of "Au Large"—who turns toward New Orleans and aspires to conform to the general patterns of American culture, deserting his picturesque way of life in favor of the "higher" culture of the Anglo-Saxon, whom Cable admires. The praise most reviewers gave the slight novel seems not undeserved, though romance and realism are hardly mixed in equal proportions, and the blend is notable for sweetness rather than potency.

There is in *Bonaventure* little direct evidence of Cable's varied activities during this period as reformer, civic leader, and lay prophet. To these avocations he gave as much of his intellectual and physical resources as to his writing and platform readings. His public appearances were as likely to be in one capacity as another, as on his two visits to Tennessee in 1887, between the magazine publication of "Grande Pointe" and "Au Large." On the first visit he read from his Acadian stories; on his second visit he read "Cobwebs in the Church" at an August meeting of the Monteagle Sunday School Assembly, a Southern Chautauqua located on a plateau in the Cumberland Mountains on land acquired from John Moffat, a temperance lecturer who was once state commissioner of immigration. Moffat's widow and daughters, who still lived at Monteagle, admired Cable's stand on Negro rights, his religious teachings, and his status as a celebrated author. Adelene Moffat, as devoted to humanitarian doctrines as her late father had been, drew a cobweb to decorate the program of Cable's lecture. He thanked the tall, pretty woman of twenty-five in a brief note, an inauspicious beginning for a correspondence and friendship that lasted nearly twenty years.

The address at Monteagle was delivered about two months after Cable had offended an audience at Vanderbilt University in Nashville by pleading the freedman's cause. Major Pond had tried to book a reading tour of the South in May, but he found it almost impossible to arrange platform appearances there because of continued hostility toward the expatriate author. Cable did make a Southern trip that month, stopping briefly in the Acadian country in the interest of "Au Large," on which he was still at work, and in New Orleans. On his way to Nashville he stopped at a number of places to study Southern conditions at first hand and to read from his works. At Fayetteville, Tennessee, he tried out the address he was to deliver at the Vanderbilt University commencement.

The invitation to speak at Vanderbilt resulted from the influence of Professor William M. Baskervill, who had consistently praised Cable as a literary genius and a credit to the South, even though the sentiments expressed in his works were not acceptable there. It was expected that Cable would speak at the university on a literary subject; instead he chose to present to what he supposed would be a particularly enlightened Southern audience his considered judgment on how the race problem might be fairly solved. In his speech, "The Faith of Our Fathers," he contended that the masses must be elevated by an effective system of free education and that the Negro must be granted full personal freedom and civil—as distinguished from social—rights. Chastened by the polite but cold reaction of the Nashville audience but undisturbed in his resolve to work for the freedman's cause, Cable carefully revised the speech that summer and published it as "The Negro Question in the United States" in New York, Chicago, and London journals in March, 1888. Had he written nothing other than this brilliant essay, which is much quoted today in discussions of minority rights, Cable's competence as a social critic would have been established beyond question.

In the correspondence that developed with Adelene Moffat, who reluctantly left Monteagle to teach at Harrison College, in Cynthiana, Kentucky, Cable reported his various activities in a manner that seems to the modern reader to reveal excessive self-esteem, although it did not impress the young woman in that way. He summarized his Bible lessons for her, gave attendance figures for his Boston and Northampton classes, and announced the schedule of his readings and speeches. Three years had elapsed since the publication of *Dr. Sevier*, and seven more would pass before he produced another novel; but because he was preoccupied with civic enterprises and reform, Cable told Adelene Moffat in October that 1887 was one of the finest years of his life. In this letter he wrote for the first time of his Home Culture Clubs, an enterprise he had begun in Northampton about a year earlier. It was as yet only a minor interest, one of far less importance to him than his involvement in the Southern problem, but it came to be his principal avocation. In his second novel, Cable said Dr. Sevier once thought that to "demolish evil" was the finest of aims, "until later years and a better self-knowledge had taught him that to do good was still finer and better." Cable was reviled for his splendid but fruitless efforts to demolish evils that the South condoned and the North looked upon with apathy. When he contented himself with merely doing good, as president of the Home Culture Clubs, he was honored as a public benefactor.

CHAPTER 7

Open Letters and Home Culture

I *Adelene Moffat*

THE CLOSING paragraphs of a long letter dated May 7, 1888, that Cable received from his young friend in Cynthiana, Kentucky, may have helped give form to a new project already in his mind or it may even have been the genesis of that project, the Open Letter Club.

It is a pity there is not some association or bureau which has for its object the clearing away of all imaginary differences in aims and hopes and which makes it an organized work to circulate every new utterance of any value on the subject of the material[,] intellectual and moral development of the South. It would be a great aid to her development in one direction at least if there were such an organization to which those of the "New South" who wish to be well informed with regard to Southern questions could apply and feel secure of receiving authentic information and through which those who are already active in Southern affairs could correspond and coöperate.

It is almost impossible for one not identified with the Southern movement to learn who is speaking and what is being said. They are dependent upon such acts of individual graciousness as the one which at present places me under obligations to you for the pamphlet on the Negro Question.[1] Thank you very much and believe me

Sincerely yours
Adelene Moffat[2]

Determined to do what he could to gain for the freedmen and the dispossessed white masses of the South the civil rights and educational opportunities they were being denied, Cable could not fail to be interested in an organization designed to serve as a clearing house for the circulation of enlightened, informative

articles on Southern problems. His extensive reading, correspondence, and travel convinced him that there were able men,
white and colored, who were giving serious thought to the issues
of the day and whose views, if made available to the public,
could help to remedy what he considered to be a deplorable
state of affairs. Cable thought that many of these men, now
silent, agreed with his own liberal views. Certainly it is true
that Cable was not alone in his opinions, nor entirely alone in
giving them public expression. But there were not many voices
crying in the wilderness during these years, and they could be
effectual only if they could be widely heard.

Adelene Moffat assured her friend she had mentioned the
idea to no one else, and they discussed its implementation in
their correspondence and then in person when she came to
Northampton to work for him in June. She spent the summer
months planning Home Culture Club work, doing research for
Cable's essays on the Negro, handling correspondence for him,
and even assisting Mrs. Cable, whom she admired, to care for
her children. There were now two Cable homes in Northampton,
for the author's mother, his sister Mary Louise, the widowed
Antoinette Cable Cox, and her three children had been brought
from New Orleans in 1886 and installed in the large "Whitcomb
House" at the corner of Park[3] and State streets. Mary Louise
rented the mansion and operated it as a boarding house for
Smith College girls. More a member of the Cable clan than an
employee, Adelene Moffat spent some of her time that summer
on the documents and manuscripts Cable published in the fall
of 1889, after their appearance in *Century Magazine,* as *Strange
True Stories of Louisiana.*

Miss Moffat did not cease to work for Cable, whom she
regarded as friend and benefactor as well as employer, when
she went to New York in September to study at the Art Students
League on a loan he arranged for her. He persuaded some two
dozen prominent men to join in a loose confederation, which he
and Adelene Moffat decided to call the Open Letter Club, but
he tried in most uncharacteristic fashion to keep his own name
out of the public record. The young woman, her sex disguised
by an "M. A. Moffat" signature, served as secretary for the
"headquarters" in New York, while William M. Baskervill filled
that role in Nashville. There was a great deal of work involved

in inducing selected persons to write articles, in duplicating these and circulating them among the members for comment, and in arranging magazine or pamphlet publication for the finished manuscripts.[4] Cable, the guiding force for the entire project, was aided by the two secretaries, friends, and relatives.

Much of the information he obtained for the Open Letter Club and for his own articles about conditions in the South was derived directly from Southern informants, white and Negro. Among the latter were Booker T. Washington, founder of Tuskegee Institute, and Charles W. Chesnutt, the only Negro member of the Open Letter Club. Chesnutt's stories in *Atlantic Monthly* led Cable to initiate a correspondence, in the course of which he not only solicited Chesnutt's collaboration with the Open Letter Club but came to serve as his literary advisor. Cable invited Chesnutt, a skilled stenographer, to be his secretary. After a visit to Northampton in March of 1889, when he took down one of Cable's Bible talks in shorthand, Chesnutt declined the secretaryship. Only because of this did Cable insist that Adelene Moffat take that post when her year of study in New York ended.

This time the young woman probably roomed at 32 Park Street and took her meals with the college girls at Mary Louise Cable's home across the street, but she continued to be on familiar terms with all the Cables at "Red House." Although at first she must have performed general secretarial services for the author, thus relieving his wife and older daughters, most of her work was with the Open Letter Club and the Home Culture Clubs. In debt to Cable for loans during the summer and the previous year, she signed a contract with him in September, 1889, which provided for an annual salary of $850 and permitted her to buy back from him—at double her rate of pay—any time she chose to devote to art.

II *Strange, True Stories*

Though romance had outweighed realism in *Bonaventure,* Cable reversed the proportion of these ingredients in his next book, *Strange True Stories of Louisiana.* For half a dozen years he had been collecting and studying family diaries, letters, court records, legal reports, and other documents which, after careful editing, comprised his true stories or were used to compose them. Intruding in the tales as translator and editor, he directed them to his social purpose, compressed at one point to improve the literary quality, and interpolated an explanation of an anachronism at another. Thus he stressed the authenticity of the narratives and made them parallels for his earlier fiction and the essays on the race problem he was publishing at this time.

Cable says in his introduction that true stories are seldom good art until, like rough gems, they have been polished by the craftsman. Yet he was so prone to rely (consciously or otherwise) on true stories as the basis for important episodes or whole plots and was so dependent on living models for his characters that critics charge him with a lack of pure creative imagination. On occasion he answered incredulous readers by assuring them that a particular character or occurrence was drawn from life—that, for example, the tiger episode in "Posson Jone'" was based on a reliable account of an actual incident or that the details of the assault on John Richling in the Parish Prison were just as he had found them in an affidavit prepared by the person who was his model for the character.[5] (Cable's claims may have a dubious value, considering that he once wrote a Boston reviewer, who had questioned the accuracy of the dialect in "Jean-ah Poquelin," that Creoles said he rendered their speech faithfully; and he added a gratuitous fabrication: "I am a creole myself."[6])

In practice, though not in printed statements about the techniques of his craft, Cable was naïve enough to suppose that verisimilitude is attained if there is a close correspondence between a reality and an author's representation of it, that the fact that his material was based on tangible truth was in itself complete justification for the use he made of that material in fiction. More than once he falls into the error of basing fiction on fact and confusing possibility with probability, a misconception that is unfortunate in *Dr. Sevier* but disastrous in *Bylow Hill*. Sometimes he gives his rough gems of truth so much polish that they have the false glitter of paste. Except for "Attalie Brouillard," however, the narratives of *Strange True Stories of Louisiana* are reconstructed with such skill that they have an impressive excellence.

Like *The Grandissimes*, Cable's true stories range over a long period of Louisiana's colorful history, the first tale being set in 1782 and one of the others depicting events that take place a century later. The stories of the early years—"The Young Aunt with White Hair," "The Adventures of Françoise and Suzanne," and "Alix de Morainville"—are fine redactions of old family documents. Vivid and thoroughly dramatic, they have a literary quality Cable did little to alter, though he contrived to make them express his equalitarian philosophy. The last piece, "War Diary of a Union Woman in the South," was one of several manuscripts he bought from Mrs. Dora Richards Miller. It turned out to be a valuable property after he abridged it severely. Published in two parts in issues of *Century Magazine* in 1885 and 1889, it was later Cable's contribution to a popular anthology, *Famous Adventures and Prison Escapes of the Civil War* (1893). Mrs. Miller was the source, too, of details about the New Orleans school he describes in "The 'Haunted House' in Royal Street." For this true story, part of which Harriet Martineau had told in *Retrospect of Western Travel* (1838), and for "Salome Müller, the White Slave," Cable was more author than editor. They are important works in his canon.

Salome Müller is the child of German immigrants who work as bond slaves in America to pay for their passage. The girl is separated from her family, and by the time relatives locate her some years later she is a grown woman and a slave unaware of her real name or identity. When they go to court to win her freedom, witnesses dismiss her appearance as inconclusive, pointing out that her owner has other slaves fairer than she who are known to be colored, if only by an infallible "instinctive means of judging" that white people in Louisiana acquire. The poor woman is finally freed on the evidence of a birthmark.

Cable uses this story to flout Southern doctrines about race and to attack slavery. His approach is that of the realist who is interested less in the possible than the probable. If one white woman could be held a slave, others may have suffered the same fate—one justifiable "alike in the law and in the popular mind" for a person of Negro extraction, however slight, but "otherwise counted hard, cruel, oppressive, and worthy of the public indignation." The case of mistaken racial identity is not employed for its romantic possibilities but for the principle involved, a principle he had already established in reverse in the octoroon stories.

"The 'Haunted House' in Royal Street" is really two different narratives. One tells of demented Madame Lalaurie's sadistic treatment of the slaves in her elegant home, later said to be haunted by the ghosts of the chained, tormented souls who burned to death in the mansion. Cable uses the story, as Harriet Martineau did, to condemn slavery. His attack in the second portion of the story shifts to the contemporary evil—segregation— he was simultaneously assailing in his essays. The restored Lalaurie house was used as a high school building during Reconstruction, when Mrs. Dora Richards Miller was a teacher there. Because it admitted both white and Negro girls, the school became a political issue.[7] In December, 1874, White Leaguers descend on the building in a mob, intent on evicting the colored pupils. As the roll is called and each girl answers to her name, those who acknowledge being colored are expelled. Some others, obviously of Negro ancestry, face down their accusers and are allowed to remain. Disclaiming any propaganda motive, Cable says, nevertheless, "Whatever the story pleads, let it plead." It is a more eloquent appeal than his articles, with their impressive array of facts, or than the two letters endorsing integrated schools which Cable wrote to the New Orleans *Bulletin* in 1875.[8]

"Attalie Brouillard," Cable admits, is unlike the other stories in the collection because its truth is attested only by oral tradition. A free quadroon, Attalie is a "worthy woman; youngish, honest, rather attractive," who keeps furnished rooms in the Vieux Carré in 1855. Cable's distaste for male quadroons is shown in his description of her friend, Camille Ducour, "narrow-chested, round-shouldered, his complexion a dull clay color spattered with large red freckles, his eyes small, gray, and close together, his hair . . . hesitating between a dull yellow and a hot red; his clothes his own and his linen last week's." Camille's smattering of law he is allowed to use in advising clients of his own caste. One of Attalie's roomers, presumably her lover, is an Englishman, a cotton buyer, whose intent to make her his sole heir seems likely to be frustrated when he dies without making a will. The shrewd free man of color takes the white man's place in bed and, before hastily summoned witnesses, executes the document Attalie needs. The deceit is detected later by friends of the Englishman, who let Attalie inherit $30,000 but see to it that Camille gets little benefit from his part in the scheme.

This tale of ante-bellum New Orleans naturally invites comparison with the stories of *Old Creole Days*. The content and manner are similar, but "Attalie Brouillard" does not equal the earlier pieces. If Cable shows again that he could not treat the male quadroon with uncritical sympathy (though Camille is degraded no more than his function in the plot requires), he also lays himself open, once more, to the charge of representing the Creole unfavorably. He renders in tedious, demeaning detail the dialect of the Creole notary public, but he gives the speech of Attalie and Camille, who use "Creole-negro *patois*," in proper English. "His head and shoulders much bundled up in wrappings," Camille might make himself look like the cotton buyer, but how he escapes detection in the deathbed scene when he speaks—in English—is not explained. Neither is the means by which the Englishman's kindly friends (who are not Creoles) discover so quickly the ruse that completely fooled the Creole eyewitnesses. "A quadroon woman's lot is a hard one," Cable says, but the story does not bear out the refrain. A slaveholder with some money and property, Attalie evidently knows all the time the value of the estate she has been promised.

No character in the tale is conceived in depth, and the action is stagey melodrama. These and other weaknesses of the story, the only one in the volume that demanded the full exercise of Cable's skill as a writer of fiction, may be significant. In the year and a half that had elapsed since the first appearance of "Au Large" and the magazine publication of "Attalie Brouillard" in September, 1889, Cable had written a wide assortment of articles on the matters to which he was devoting all the time he could spare from his work as a platform reader: Bible study and teaching, the Home Culture Clubs, and Negro rights. So involved was he in the concerns of the Open Letter Club that the novel he began in the spring of 1889 seemed even to him to bear too close a resemblance to his essays and lay sermons. Busy with civic affairs and public controversies and no longer a citizen of New Orleans, he was at this time little interested in the romantic aspects of old Creole Louisiana.

III *Noble Social Aims*

He was, on the other hand, increasingly concerned about his Home Culture Clubs, to which Adelene Moffat, as general secretary (really general manager), was now devoting most of her time. Probably Cable thought the basic concept of the project was his own, though he recognized that there were some similar undertakings in operation, and he admitted that he was not unwilling to appropriate whatever promised to be useful. Much he borrowed, consciously and unconsciously, for the main idea of his scheme was circulating in the air all about him. There was widespread interest in home study and in improvement of the home: *Good Housekeeping*, designed "For the Homes of the World," began publication in nearby Holyoke, Massachusetts, in May, 1885, when Cable was on the verge of moving to Northampton, and was published in Holyoke until 1910; the first issue of the *Ladies' Journal*, which appeared in December, 1883, had a logotype depicting a fireside scene labeled "Home," and its title soon became the *Ladies' Home Journal.* But the fact that Cable's enterprise was unoriginal and eclectic is of little importance in assessing its significance.

Speculation about the source of the name Cable selected is easily resolved. It was his practice to read the quality magazines of his day with care, and certainly *Scribner's Monthly* for October, 1873, which he must have read from cover to cover, made a lasting impression upon him. " 'Sieur George," his first work in a national magazine, appeared near the back of that issue; immediately following the story were the editorials, the first of which announced the founding of Smith College. Just as the item on the new college, born at the moment of his entry into the world of letters, stirred Cable's imagination and, very probably, influenced his settling in Northampton a dozen years later, so did other material on those back pages linger in his mind. One of the magazine's departments was titled "Home and Society" and another, the book reviews, was called "Culture and Progress." The two headings, hyphenated into "Home-Culture," gave Cable the name for his clubs and perhaps something more, for "Society" was the end the clubs were to serve and "Progress" the result they were to achieve.

Initially the clubs were small groups of people who gathered at private homes to read aloud from books of their own selection. The idea was to stimulate home study and personal growth among culturally impoverished families. While the spires of the churches and college buildings rose grandly at one end of Northampton, factory chimneys dominated the other. The social classes of the little city ran to similar extremes, and there was little social contact between them. The immigrants and other culturally underprivileged people would benefit, Cable thought, from reading and from association with educated members of the community who served as club leaders.

The first public meeting of the clubs was held in May, 1887, when Smith professor John H. Pillsbury gave a lecture, "Pond Life," illustrated with the stereopticon. Pillsbury was one of the members of the Northampton Social and Literary Club, whose members may have given Cable ideas for the development of his project. Others of the "twelve apostles" were early supporters of the enterprise, and four of them became trustees when it was formally organized as the Home Culture Clubs Company in 1896. In January of 1888 there were fourteen clubs and over a hundred members. Cable discussed the project at a public meeting in the Opera House, at which the mayor and the president of Smith College, L. Clarke Seelye, praised the clubs as an effort to break down such social barriers as served no useful purpose.

Cable's article in *Century Magazine* the following August was cautious in expounding the social aims of the program; it has the mannered style of his Creole fiction rather than the forceful and direct approach of his essays on education, prison reform, and the rights of the freedmen. He stressed the number of pages read and the values of self-improvement without indicating precisely how his benevolent project would contribute in any significant way to improve the status or elevate the cultural level of the masses. Over the years that followed, however, it did indeed perform noble public service in Northampton, an accomplishment that must be credited to the devoted management of Adelene Moffat as much as to the leadership of the founder.

Adelene Moffat assumed responsibility for the project, under Cable's direction, in the fall of 1889. Since he was often away from Northampton on reading engagements, he had to manage much of his Open Letter Club and Home Culture Club business by correspondence. The letters he and Adelene Moffat exchanged over the twenty-year period of their relationship constitute an illuminating record of his personality and character and are important sources of information about his personal and public affairs. Unlike the general run of his correspondence, these letters, many of them dashed off in careless haste, were not written with an eye to posterity, though they were sometimes careful and calculating efforts to accomplish some specific objective. Cable's petty vanities, his expedient forgetfulness, and his bland disregard for inconvenient facts may be read between the lines—lines that also verify his achievements as reformer, social critic, and civic benefactor.

Almost from the beginning of the correspondence Cable's letters reveal traits that were to be crucial to the relationship in later years. Once he sent the young woman fifty dollars due on her salary that he said he had forgotten to pay her before he left Northampton. Despite his notorious forgetfulness, the explanation is as dubious as his statement on another occasion that a telegram from him had reached her "collect" because of the mistake of a stranger. Cable's chronic lack of funds resulted from a financial condition so complicated and precarious as to encourage constant borrowing from Peter to pay Paul. He and Adelene Moffat were continually in debt to one another, a state of affairs that worked more to Cable's ultimate advantage than to hers. Among the children with whom the older Cable girls were on friendly terms were three of the Brewster girls, daughters of a Northampton florist, who sometimes found their father's bills scattered on the floor of the Cable home. The bills were paid, as were the others that piled up, but not with scrupulous punctuality. Unpaid bills worried Mrs. Cable but did not greatly disturb her husband.

Mark Twain was infuriated by the professed and active piety of the G. W. Cable who was his companion on the reading tour of 1884-85, but Twain would have found Cable's relaxed practices and liberal opinions of a dozen years later relatively inoffensive. For Cable, one highlight of that tour had been, at its close, the day when he finally prevailed on Twain to accompany him to church. The decline of Cable's religious fervor may be traced in his fiction and is reflected in his letters to Adelene Moffat. The earliest letters were often little sermons presenting his interpretation of scripture or theological doctrine. Many of these letters closed with "God Bless You." In the 1890's this became "Good Fortune to you," interesting evidence of Cable's adjustment to the materialistic emphasis of the time. The religious tone became infrequent in his letters, except for those written on Sundays, and at last it virtually disappeared.

But in the first two or three years of his association with Adelene Moffat, Cable was thoroughly devoted to the religious and social projects in which he was engaged, and their association rested on a firm foundation of compatibility of interests. Cable, who had made drawings in his notebooks since Civil War days, had long been attracted to art and had an intelligent understanding of Adelene Moffat's studies and ambitions. Some of his children were pupils in the art classes she started soon after moving to Northampton. Like her father, who was born in Scotland, Adelene Moffat had always been out of sympathy with Southern racial attitudes, and she wholeheartedly endorsed Cable's sacrificial efforts to persuade the nation to grant civil rights to the Negro. In Northampton she soon demonstrated a quality that Cable entirely lacked, a talent for working with the kind of people with whom he concerned himself when he read his paper, "The Improvement of the Common People," at a meeting of the Northampton Social and Literary Club on April 19, 1888. His proclivities were in the direction of social theory and organizational planning; his was an impersonal benevolence. His chief concern at this time was the vexing Negro problem, not Northampton's uncultured masses. When his turn to lead the Club's discussions came in February of 1889, he was back on the subject that obsessed him: "The Social and Political Problem of the South."

On his tour of the West that fall, Cable's platform readings were less on his mind than his crusade. Early in November he had tea with Charles W. Chesnutt at his home in Cleveland and discussed with him plans for the Open Letter Club. About two weeks later when he wrote Adelene Moffat from Erie to tell her to do all she could "night and day" to promote the interests of the Home Culture Clubs, he mentioned a donation of $500 from Alfred T. Lilly. A businessman and philanthropist of Florence, Massachusetts, Lilly had given Florence the Lilly Library the year before, and two years earlier he had donated funds for the Smith College Lilly Hall of Science. When he died in 1890 he left to the Florence Kindergarten money that was used to provide free classes in manual training and domestic science. Florence thus set a precedent of free adult education, with an emphasis on practical training, that Cable's Home Culture Clubs soon followed in Northampton.

December found Cable again in Nashville, not as a Vanderbilt speaker this time but to see Baskervill and to read from his works at Ward's Seminary. On a brief appearance at Fisk University, whose Negro students and liberal teachers had long admired his forthright advocacy of their cause, he spoke with discretion. After that, he made what Baskervill, his Nashville host, recognized as a serious tactical error. In pursuit of information for his Open Letter Club, he met a number of colored people at the home of James C. Napier, a prominent Negro, and "broke bread" with them. This flagrant violation of the Southern code laid Cable open to the charge of endorsing social rather than merely civil equality. The press in Nashville and elsewhere in the South attacked him violently. Even his friends were disappointed, for one reason or another, with the spirited defense he made in reply. The damage to the already shaky Open Letter Club was irreparable. Members found it expedient to withdraw, and the project, Cable's most ambitious and selfless effort to aid the underprivileged masses of the South, quickly died.

His enthusiasm for the cause of the freedman waned after this, as did his idealism in general and his confidence in the efficacy of public discussion to resolve controversial national issues. He never quite recovered from this failure to awaken the nation's conscience and direct it, through dispassionate reasoning, to a solution of what he regarded as the most crucial problem of the times. He had manuscripts in progress, based on his studies of the predicament of the Negro and the poor white, and for two or three years he continued to speak his mind on these subjects. But gradually he retreated from the extremes of his early demands for full equality for the freedman and at last fell silent altogether, except for what social criticism and political liberalism—weakened by his own ambiguity and indirection and by his publisher's censorship—appeared in his fiction. He had called the Open Letter Club "the dear good work" in his letters to Adelene Moffat. After the Napier incident, "the dear good work" always meant the Home Culture Clubs.

CHAPTER 8

Johnny Reb

I *Miscellaneous Writings*

BEFORE RETURNING home from Nashville in December, 1889, Cable stopped at Monteagle and left questions to be answered by Adelene Moffat's oldest sister, Mrs. Jennie Weir. The inquiries were related to the novel on which he was at work, a treatment of Reconstruction and post-Reconstruction in the South. Just as he had made *Dr. Sevier* a vehicle for condemning New Orleans prisons, he hoped to incorporate in his new book his ideas about solutions to problems facing the contemporary South. But Cable's editors, Richard Watson Gilder in particular, were now even more averse to reform and social criticism than they had been a decade earlier. Cable maintained his friendship with Gilder, although the strain of their many differences of opinion led him to say to Adelene Moffat that Gilder made him sick. The editor was thoroughly displeased with the manuscript for two magazine installments Cable had completed by July, 1890. Cable was writing a tract, Gilder felt, not literature. It was several revisions and four years later before installments of the novel, *John March, Southerner*, began to appear, and then not in Gilder's *Century* but in *Scribner's Magazine*.

When the American Missionary Association met in Northampton in October, 1890, Cable delivered an address—a revision of a talk, "The South's First Needs," he had made in Washington on May 16, under the auspices of Howard University—in which he said that education for the Negro must not be confined primarily to manual, domestic, and industrial training. He had learned not to bring to an audience opinions it did not wish to hear. The position he took in his speech differed with that of Booker T. Washington and the Northern philanthropists whose contributions were the source of the Negro leader's increasing influence, but it was in complete accord with the policies of Howard University and the American Missionary Association. The American Missionary Association published the address as a pamphlet, *What the Negro Must Learn.*

Among the educational institutions supported by the association was Berea College, which had been founded by Kentucky abolitionists and operated for years as an interracial school and to which Roswell Smith contributed about $50,000. Following his venerated friend's lead, Cable visited Berea several times, spoke at commencement, and praised its work wherever and whenever he could. At the request of the widow of the man who had been his most active patron, he wrote *A Memory of Roswell Smith* in 1892. The book expresses warm admiration for the publisher, political liberal, Congregationalist layman, and philanthropist who was his staunch friend. Cable, who wanted the world to regret him when he died, hoped to attain for himself a reputation like that of Roswell Smith.

With this memorial volume, Cable's period of miscellaneous writing came to an end. In 1889, Scribner's had issued a new edition of *The Silent South* which included open letters in which Cable had defended the original essays. Six articles he had published in various journals were collected in *The Negro Question* in 1890.[1] "My Politics," an essay he intended to include in the volume, was held, on the advice of his editors, for posthumous publication.[2] Most of the articles in *The Negro Question* were related to Cable's abortive Open Letter Club, which was also the general source of a few additional items that came out in periodicals after publication of the book. The last of these articles—its title indicative of Cable's broadened approach to Southern issues and suggestive of his withdrawal from the controversy on Negro rights—was "Education for the Common People in the South" which appeared in the *Cosmopolitan* of November, 1892.

Cable made no further frontal assaults on the Southern philosophy and practices he deplored. The death of the Open Letter Club had dispelled his illusion that the South would listen to dispassionate debate on controversial subjects and would heed the advice of high-minded men who urged the adoption of a course of action based on principle rather than on expediency. And he recognized that the spread of discrimination, the indifference of Northern liberals, and the triumph of white supremacy doctrines in the New South spelled the doom of the ex-slave's hopes to attain the rights of full citizenship. Yet he could not refrain from crowding into the novel he was writing at this time some expression of his own equalitarian philosophy, however watered down and disguised, and from hoping that the book might have a beneficial influence on national and sectional policy. His campaign to obtain civil rights for the Negro (which, of course, did not have his exclusive attention at any time) had its origin in his rejection of the pernicious Bible defense of slavery years earlier and was not unrelated to his religious principles. Therefore, it is not surprising, that his political and religious writings came to an end at about the same time. He had ceased to conduct Bible classes; and, after the publication in 1891 of *The Busy Man's Bible,* a collection of the short pieces he had been doing for several years on how to teach and study the Bible, he wrote no more about church policy or about interpretation of the scriptures. Cable's period of spiritual emphasis and sacrificial devotion to noble causes was over.

II *Real Estate and Classes*

A turning point in his life occurred in August, 1890, when he and a partner bought Paradise Woods, about six acres of land near Smith College, at Paradise Road and Washington Avenue. Two summers later, when he was $4,000 in debt to the Century Company, he sold some lots but bought additional land, the Ward Tract, on Paradise Road. Cable bought a house that had stood on Elm Street, moved it to the corner of Dryads' Green and Harrison Avenue, and remodeled it; he preferred to say he built it. It was ready for the family to move into early in 1892 after Cable's return from his second reading tour of the West Coast. This home, which he named "Tarryawhile," was a source of immense satisfaction to him. It was material evidence of his success, a proper setting in which to entertain Northampton associates and visiting notables, and an appropriate residence for a nationally famous author and a man winning a reputation in his city as a public benefactor. He moved to his new property the souvenir trees that celebrities had planted for him a few hundred yards away at "Red House," and he directed the development of the beautiful woods and garden that sloped down to Paradise Lake, known to a later and more blasé generation of college girls as "Passion Puddle." To Cable, it was delightful to have an opportunity to indulge his love for flowers and gardens.

But neither his involved real estate transactions—one daughter said, "Father bought a hill and a hole and put the hill into the hole and sold it for building lots"[3]—nor his gardening distracted Cable from his interest in the Home Culture Clubs. For some time Adelene Moffat, as general secretary, had prepared reports on the clubs, many of them located outside Northampton. These statements of the titles of books and the number of pages read at meetings were of little value in describing or promoting the enterprise, which was no longer merely a loose confederation of fireside reading clubs. The new direction the work had taken may be seen in the monthly publication, *Home Culture Club Letter*, which began to appear in 1892. The first issue, for September, carried a list of suggested readings and a digest of Cable's remarks to the club leaders at their first monthly meeting of the new season. On the first page, under "Secretary's Notes," it was announced that there was room for new members in certain clubs, among which were the following:

> Boys' Arithmetic
> Girls' Gymnastic
> Young Ladies' Gymnastic
> Advanced French
> Young Men's History
> Young Men's English Composition
> Men's Book-keeping

From this list, it is clear that these were not reading clubs; they were classes. The first steps in this direction had been taken inadvertently in the spring of 1888 when rooms over a Main Street department store were rented to serve as head-quarters and as a convenience for men who had no homes or whose homes were unsuitable for club meetings. Shelves were stocked with books and magazines, and the rooms were left open at night. Sometime after Adelene Moffat came to work with the clubs in 1889, she found that boys and young men off the street had virtually appropriated the reading room as a lounge. Their interest in the prize ring, fighting, and battles she channeled into informal group study of the American Revolution. This led naturally to a class in citizenship and, for older men, to discussion of Bryce's *American Commonwealth*.

There was at Smith College a group of girls who belonged to the International Order of King's Daughters and Sons, a non-denominational service organization. When the King's Daughters volunteered to aid the Home Culture Clubs, Adelene Moffat decided that the most practical way of using their assistance, and that of other Smith students, was in further development of the classes. Women and girls were admitted to the study groups, and from this time on the college girls contributed their services as teachers. Enough of them participated in the work in 1891-92 to warrant a comment from President Seelye in his annual report on the college; thereafter there is abundant record of their activity as teachers for the clubs.

It was Adelene Moffat who made it possible for Cable to combine his interest in Smith College with his sponsorship of the Home Culture Clubs. He was often seen on Smith's campus, but his appearances there were as a writer rather than as a social critic, reformer, or philanthropist. He read to the college girls from his works on February 13, 1886; introduced a lecture on Russia on October 16, 1889; and again read from his works to the literary society on May 16, 1890. Once he talked to a large group on an unusual but refreshingly unacademic subject: "Be Happy." Never, it seems, did he address the students formally in behalf of any of his causes.

During these years Adelene Moffat ate her meals and lived with Smith girls, whose work as volunteer teachers for church groups and women's clubs she admired. She symbolized the Home Culture Clubs to the girls, who were inspired by her but somewhat awed by Cable when he addressed the monthly meetings of club leaders. The study groups meeting at the headquarters were called "clubs," and it was years before Cable understood and acknowledged, reluctantly, that his scheme for promoting fireside reading among the culturally underprivileged had become a community service agency engaged in a systematic program of adult education. This development would have been impossible without the generosity of Edward H. R. Lyman, a retired businessman who had given Northampton its Academy of Music[4] and had contributed heavily toward building the city's library resources. Through Lyman the Home Culture Clubs obtained the old Methodist Church on Center Street in 1893. When the two-story building was remodeled to serve as a clubhouse for its new occupants, it had an assembly room seating four hundred, a well-equipped stage on the second floor, and accommodations for nearly a hundred classes a week.

III *John March, Southerner*

A month after the publication of his final essay on Southern problems, Cable found himself involved in another controversy —this time a personal one. The source of several of the narratives he had published as *Strange True Stories of Louisiana* was Mrs. Dora Richards Miller, a New Orleans school teacher who had literary aspirations. He had small success in his efforts to help her place her work in the magazines, but he paid her for research and he bought from her a diary she had kept as a Union sympathizer during the Civil War, as has already been noted, and another manuscript reporting her childhood experiences during an insurrection in 1848. Offended because he did not name her as the writer of "A West Indian Slave Insurrection" when it appeared in *Scribner's Magazine* in December, 1892, Mrs. Miller announced her claims as author in a letter to the New Orleans *Times-Democrat*. Various journals circulated charges that Cable had exploited Mrs. Miller and misled the public. In his letter to the *Critic*, February 4, 1893, he pointed out that he had paid Mrs. Miller for her manuscripts, had revised them extensively, and had identified himself as editor rather than as author. She answered in the same journal in March, but Cable did not continue the dispute. Evidently convinced that his part in the matter was an honorable one, he incorporated the story in one of his last novels and also made later use of other materials he had obtained from Mrs. Miller. His reputation for fair dealing, however, did not emerge unscathed from the controversy.

Much of Cable's income was derived, as it had been for years, from his platform readings from his works. These were now polished but routine. The program for his appearance at the

Union Congregational Church in Providence, Rhode Island, on January 4, 1892, was typical: two selections, including the classroom scene, were from "Grande Pointe"; one from "Au Large"; and three from *Dr. Sevier*, closing with "Mary's Night Ride" as a climax. Occasionally he gave readings with other authors, and in the winter of 1892-93 he made a tour of the East and Midwest with Eugene Field. It was a pleasant experience but lacking in the satisfactions and excitement of the tour with Mark Twain.

Platform readings took his time, but not his attention. He was busy writing fiction again, and the Home Culture Clubs were much on his mind. A new activity, the production of plays, was being undertaken by some of the club members. When they presented Howells' *A Letter of Introduction* in April, Cable wrote to remind Adelene Moffat that shy Howells, who was his house guest, was not to be expected to attend the amateur production. Cable, now a devotee of the theater, was an enthusiastic supporter of the dramatic activities at the clubhouse, where another Howells farce, *The Garroters* (later renamed *A Dangerous Ruffian*) was presented the following winter.

"The Taxidermist," Cable's first story in five years, appeared in *Scribner's Magazine* in May, 1893. Richard Watson Gilder rejected *John March, Southerner* in June, for the third time. The version Cable completed in August was accepted by *Scribner's Magazine*, the first installment being published in January, 1894, ten years after the first installments of *Dr. Sevier*, Cable's last novel, had come out.

He had changed, not merely aged, during that decade. Although *John March, Southerner* is a product of his long crusade for a progressive, democratic South, there is abundant evidence in the book that by the time the final version was completed he had not only withdrawn from the controversies of the 1880's but had accommodated his literary and political principles to meet the demands of editors, readers, and society in general. In his first talk before the members of the Northampton Social and Literary Club in 1886, Cable spoke on "The Southern Question," and some aspect of this subject was his topic at club meetings in 1889, 1890, and 1891; but the next year he chose to lead a discussion which safely explored "Art in the West," and his uncontroversial subject in 1893 was "Morality in Literature." Such a compromise was not new in Cable's life, for, when he was writing *Dr. Sevier*, he had brought his reason, his inclination, and his practical interests to bear to free himself from the family tradition that pronounced attendance at the theater morally wrong. Ten years later, with their older daughters at a marriageable age, he and his wife escaped from another inconvenient dogma by deciding that social dancing was not sinful either. When the oldest girl, Louise, married James A. Chard in December, 1894, Cable rented a large cottage opposite his house for the occasion. There was a reception for four hundred guests, an elaborate supper was served in the evening, and the dancing that began about nine o'clock "lasted to a late hour."[5]

When Cable was writing *Old Creole Days* and *The Grandissimes* he was convinced that literature must have an underlying moral purpose, that it should be both elevating and instructive. When he began *John March, Southerner* he thought of the book as an agent for demolishing evil, for turning the South and the nation as a whole from the pernicious abridgment of the rights of the Negro citizen. (Why might not a novel do for the freedman what *Uncle Tom's Cabin* had done for the slave?) But he received no encouragement from the Century Company and, his account heavily overdrawn, he could not afford to ignore the disheartening objections of the magazine's editors. In the years that had passed since the publication of "The Freedman's Case in Equity" and Grady's "In Plain Black and White," more than one issue of *Century Magazine* had endorsed Grady's stand and opposed Cable's. Now Gilder responded to each draft of the new book, first called *Johnny Reb* and then *Widewood*, with pronounced displeasure. Cable should beware the fate of Tolstoy, Gilder said, and compared his friend's work with the polemics of Albion Tourgée. The editor asked for more books like "beautiful" *Bonaventure*.

As one draft after another was rejected as a tract by Gilder and as the campaign for Negro rights met rebuff after rebuff, Cable was led to rationalize his literary philosophy and to conclude that the primary purpose of fiction must be entertainment. This view he did not fully reconcile with his original opinion that a novel might legitimately be a political work with a moral effect strong enough to nourish the soul. As a result, *John March, Southerner* turned out to be neither fish nor fowl.

Yet it may be, as has been said in a recent appraisal, that it is "the most interesting novel" Cable ever wrote.[6] It is important in literary history as one of the earliest serious novels about the South in the years immediately after the Civil War by a Southerner who had observed Reconstruction and its aftermath; who had studied the period with intelligence, industry, and objectivity; and who could write of the times as both scholar and artist. And like other books by Cable, it has interesting biographical implications.

John March, Southerner reveals a good deal about the changing religious position of a man too generally categorized as a zealous puritan throughout the course of his life. Cable's early portraits of clergymen had been inherently kindly and respectful. He was a fervent Presbyterian when, in "Posson Jone'," he showed a gullible Baptist parson brought to grief by the wiles of Jules St.-Ange and a drink he thought was lemonade, but Cable made the minister a genuinely devout man untainted by hypocrisy. Though there are slurs on Catholicism in the Creole fiction, Cable did not question the sincerity of its worshipers, whom he considered misguided, at worst; and he made Père Jerome in *Madame Delphine* an unblemished Creole hero. Religious convictions give added strength to several important characters in *Dr. Sevier* and *Bonaventure,* and practical Christianity motivates the noble acts of Kristian Koppig and Joseph Frowenfeld. But religion plays no such role in *John March, Southerner,* whose hero is a convert to the new national faith—materialism—and whose villain is a minister of the gospel. Two years before Harold Frederic published *The Damnation of Theron Ware,* Cable dared to depict a preacher as a lecher and a hypocrite, a man who slaps his teen-age daughter and tells her she may not do as she "damn pleases."

A former circuit rider, Major Garnet is founder and president of Rosemont College. As a respected leader of the town of "Suez" in "the State of Dixie," he lends his authority to the catchwords of the New South. When at last Garnet is exposed as a land speculator, an embezzler, and an adulterer, he leaves Suez in disgrace to become a "platform star" who is famous in the North as "the eloquent Southern orator, moralist and humorist" who lectures on "Temptation and How to Conquer It." This light fate seems a violation of poetic justice, but it may be that Cable chose it with all the deliberation of Dante assigning torments to sinners in hell. Garnet is a complex character, as human as he is despicable. So are the other swindlers, drunkards, and opportunists, all of them citizens of the world as much as residents of Cable's "State of Dixie."

Dashing Jeff-Jack Ravenal, once Major Garnet's adjutant and later his partner in chicanery, is no more the conventional Confederate veteran than is General Halliday, who wins political office by collaborating with the Reconstruction government. No innocent Southern belle, the general's daughter Fannie is a sophisticated woman of the world, who proves her mettle when she locks drunken Jeff-Jack out of her Pullman compartment on their wedding night. Cornelius Leggett is a debauched Negro politician but not an unmitigated scoundrel; paradoxically, he schemes for schools for Negroes and poor whites as well as for money to line his own pockets. As vicious in her own way as any villain in the book is John March's selfish mother, through whom Cable ridicules the simpering sentimentality of the Southern "poetess" and strikes at the religious pretensions he could abide no more in a sanctimonious Southern matron than in the Bible students he had once taught in Boston, whose "average religion" he decried as "water-logged with last century bilge-water."[7]

The preacher who is a foil for Garnet is venerable Parson Tombs, well meaning but ineffectual. Asked to hold revival meetings at his church and to admit Negro students to the gallery, he seeks the approval of his church board. Cable puts in the mouth of one board member the doctrine he had propounded in an article, "Congregational Unity in Georgia," published on September 26, 1889, in *Congregationalist*: "I jes know if my Lawd an' Master was here in Dixie now he'd not bless a single one of all these separations between churches, aw in churches," the man says, and he proposes that the students be allowed to sit anywhere. Major Garnet argues that admitting Negroes, even to the gallery, would "create dissension—in a church where everything now is as sweet and peaceful as the grave." "Of course we mustn't have dissensions," Parson Tombs replies.

Cable could not avoid putting into this novel, his first in ten years, something of what he had learned about people who had his sympathy but whose human failings he had learned from his broadened experience. The book does not idealize ministers, or Confederate veterans, or women, or Negroes, all of whom Cable had treated gently in his earlier writing, and it depicts the real motive of politicians and entrepreneurs as personal aggrandizement. The hero, a blundering quick-tempered, confused, fallible young man, is quite unlike the self-righteous and guiltless protagonists who preceded him. Cable's old New Orleans was exotic; his "State of Dixie" is sordid. His antagonist is not society in the abstract; it is a composite of assorted ignoble human beings beset by a variety of problems and driven by base personal compulsions—sex, greed, alcohol—far more than by regional behavior patterns. *John March, Southerner* is not a polemic; it is a kind of confession.

Cable's personal integrity was on the decline. No longer a purveyor of "sweetness and light" sacrificing his private interests in his devotion to altruism, he was now a practical realist inclined to give to his real estate maneuvers in Northampton time he would once have spent in Bible teaching or in writing essays on Negro rights. He had made a sharp contract with Adelene Moffat soon after he began *John March, Southerner*, and before it was finished he had to defend himself against Mrs. Miller's complaints about his use of her manuscripts. His mother, who was the source of many of his ideals, was dead; his sister's family, the Coxes, had begun to leave Northampton; his own children were beginning to scatter from his home. He was no longer a Sabbatarian. The traveling man becomes a cosmopolite, and Cable, who had been lecturing and reading from his works for a decade, made two trips to the West Coast while he was writing *John March, Southerner*.

His inclination to rely on fact as the basis for fiction had not changed, though he knew the dangers of this procedure and advised others against following it. For example, he warned Charles W. Chesnutt, at work on an early draft of *The House Behind the Cedars*, to present the truth in his fiction but not actual occurrences. But Cable could not follow his own advice when a story came to his hand that seemed too good to ignore. Adelene Moffat's late father, "Colonel" John Moffat, was once the owner of a very large tract of land on Cumberland Mountain in Tennessee. He was responsible for bringing immigrants to settle in the state to promote its industrial development. With his help two Southern ladies established a girls' school, Fairmount, on the Cumberland plateau, where he had hoped to found his own collegiate and normal institute. Financial reverses drove him back to the platform as a temperance lecturer and led him to sell part of his land as a site for the Monteagle Sunday School Assembly, at which Cable spoke in 1887. By that time John Moffat was dead, but the story of the loss of his estate through the duplicity of his partner and a mix-up in deeds was surely still in circulation.

John Moffat's career in Tennessee provided the basis for Cable's plot. When John March inherits a vast tract of land from his father, he attempts to colonize and industrialize the region. Most of March's neighbors oppose his plans for one reason or another, and those who pretend to be his friends exert themselves to fleece him of his interests. He is saved from the villainy of Major Garnet only when Barbara Garnet's dream reveals that, because of a mistake in the deeds, her father's college is built on land that belongs to March.

Cable could have heard Moffat's story from Moffat's relatives, first his admirers and later his friends, who were his guides and who supplied information for his notes. He made more than one trip to Monteagle, the town Moffat had founded a hundred miles southeast of Nashville. Adelene Moffat was at hand in Northampton to fill in details about the mountaineers, the schools, the possibilities for industrial development, the conflicts among the different factions in the area. What she told Cable about her father, whom she deeply admired, suggested qualities he assigned to Judge March, the hero's father. Cable used Moffat's widow, and perhaps his eldest daughter, to create the sanctimonious Mrs. March. The Fairmount school Moffat aided becomes Montrose Academy in the novel, a sister institution to Major Garnet's Rosemont. When the conventional heroine, Barbara Garnet, goes to Smith College to finish her education, Cable sets some scenes in Paradise Woods, adjacent to his new home, but he refrains from naming the institution or the New England college town, which he employs for its typicality rather than its particulars.

He does not limit himself to all the specifics of the Moffat story in building his plot, and he breaks away from the local color techniques he had used in his earlier writing. In order to treat the entire South, he pointedly avoids the setting and character types associated with his fiction. Louisiana, with its Creoles, Acadians, and quadroons, had a unique history and special problems that made it inappropriate for his purpose. From his notes on widely scattered locales, he created a physical and political geography that has a greater significance and a more compelling reality than could have been achieved by a transcription of actuality. The dialect follows a regional speech pattern, generally commonplace, sometimes theatrical, but never picturesque. In the tradition of local color, Cable's early protagonists were always outsiders—a Dutchman or German or pious Kentuckian in the Latin culture of New Orleans, a Creole or Yankee in the Acadian Bayou Têche, an abolitionist in the slave South, a puritan narrator in a Catholic world. John March, however, is a native of Dixie, an insider who represents in his person the prejudices, aspirations, limitations, and strengths of his society. The book is not local color, nor a historical novel, nor a defense of the plantation tradition, all of which it has been called. It is rather Cable's nearest approach to regionalism.

That *John March, Southerner* does not measure up to the standards of this genre cannot be denied, but, in view of the editorial opposition to early drafts of the book and the romantic preferences of the magazine-reading public, it is hard now to say where the blame for the failure lies. In any case, the failure is as interesting as the accomplishment. Cable got into the book, as Randolph Bourne said, "pretty nearly the entire life of a turbulent and proud Southern community in its welter of personal and political feuds and aspirations to develop its suddenly discovered resources."[8] Holding his didactic nature in check, he veiled his doctrines in ambiguity and made his characters "vivid portraits which were the reverse of special pleading for the sociological idealism he had been expressing."[9] By adopting the objectivity of the social historian, Cable robbed the book of the strength he had given *The Grandissimes* by making that work a direct and emotional expression of his convictions. He burdened *John March, Southerner* with an unduly involved main plot heavily dependent upon contrived coincidences, dream revelation, and the exposition of a narrator who intrudes in the closing pages. And, bowing to the practices that had become standard at the time, he descended to minstrelsy and stereotyping in presenting Negro character.

Cable was once so sensitive to "nigger" that he persuaded Mark Twain to change the title of one of his readings from "You Can't Teach a Nigger to Argue" to "How Come a Frenchman Doan' Talk Like a Man?" so that the printed program might not be "the faintest bit gross."[10] He had used "nigger" and "darky" very sparingly in his Louisiana books, and then only in dialogue. In *John March, Southerner,* however, these appellations are employed more generally. The physical appearance of some of the numerous colored characters is treated as a source of humor, as when Cable speaks of the "red cavern" of Aunt Virginia's mouth and sees the blackness of certain other Negroes as ludicrous. Aunt Virginia and her husband, Uncle Leviticus, are duplicates of the myriad "aunts" and "uncles" in plantation idylls stretching from J. P. Kennedy's *Swallow Barn* (1832) to Thomas Nelson Page's *In Ole Virginia* (1887); Page and his followers won a literary victory that did much to nullify the ceremonies at Appomattox Courthouse, and Cable bowed to the weight of superior numbers.[11]

Cable makes Aunt Virginia's son, Cornelius Leggett, one of his major characters, a mulatto *deus ex machina,* but he uses him for comic relief in the minstrel tradition. Drunkard, bigamist, and blackmailer, "School-house Leggett" is a sharp businessman and an astute politician. Cable has him speak an outlandish stage dialect that makes it difficult to take him seriously or to identify his statements as paraphrases of passages in Cable's earlier essays on the race question. "White man ain't eveh goin' to lif hisseff up by holdin' niggeh down," Leggett tells John March. He descends from sage to buffoon when he adds, "an' that's the pyo chaotic truth; now, ain't it?"

"Best way is to hang the nigger up."
"Aw, Mr. March, you a-jokin'! You know I espress the truth. Ef you wants to make a rich country, you ain't got to make it a white man's country, naw a black man's country, naw yit mix the races an' make it a yaller man's country, much less a

yaller woman's; no, seh! But the whole effulgence is jess this:
you got to make it a po' man's country! Now, you accentuate
yo' reflections on that, seh!"

No country without free schools for all can be good for poor
men, black or white, Leggett argues, as Cable had done for
years. But Leggett is an ineffectual spokesman for the author,
since Cable never ratifies his pronouncements. And all Leggett
asks for his people is "separate but equal" education, not full
civil rights.

The book has no *raisonneur*. John March is a more convincing
protagonist than the excessively noble heroes of Cable's other
novels, but the particular human frailties that make him seem
real also reduce his stature so drastically as to prevent him from
personifying large principles. March's problem is how to hold
and use his father's legacy, not how to save the South.
Widewood,[12] the tract of a hundred thousand acres he inherits,
will be the source of his fortune, he believes, if it can be
colonized and its industrial potential exploited.[13] March, who
grows up in a bigoted community passing through the trials of
Reconstruction into the triumph of the New South, not only
sees but approves the re-establishment of white supremacy, the
imposition of segregation, the disfranchisement of the poor man.
Dixie will prosper, March reasons, if Northerners will provide
capital without supposing their money gives them the right to
offer idealistic political advice. By the time his personal affairs
end happily when he wins Barbara Garnet, March, having
learned to control his impetuosity and to make the most of his
meager intellectual resources, has become a leader in his community, a practical and conservative man whose good will is
tempered by loyalty to his section and his class. Cable had once
scorned an industrialized, commercialized South that violated
fundamental precepts of democratic government, but it is such
a South his hero epitomizes. One of March's friends remarks
that he has become a "very fine" influence, though prone to feel
the community does not "do the dahkeys justice." But, he asks,
"When it comes to that, seh, where on earth *does* the under
man get all his rights?" The rhetorical question is allowed to
stand as the South's defense, not its apologia.

A few years earlier, in "The Southern Struggle for Pure

Government" (in which he said, "On the race question I am a Republican; on some others I am a Democrat, and on all questions I know and am ready to avow exactly where I stand. . . ."), Cable had been severely critical of the New South that John March represents.

We are reminded that "in the South there are Negro lawyers, teachers, editors, dentists, doctors and preachers working in peace and multiplying with the increasing ability of their race to support them." But whence came they? Nine-tenths of those teachers and preachers and ninety-nine hundredths of those lawyers, editors, dentists and doctors have got their professions in colleges built and sustained by Northern money, and taught by Northern missionary teachers whom the great bulk of this New South rewards with social ostracism. They work in peace. But what a peace! A peace bought by silent endurance of a legalized system of arrogant incivilities that make them, in almost every public place, conspicuous objects of a public disdain which is not always even silent. What single one of those tyrannous and vulgar intrusions of private social selection into purely public places, has this New South of iron and coal mines, and new railways and cotton mills, and oil-presses removed? Not one! From the ennobling relaxations of the drama, the opera, the oratorio, the orchestral symphony and sonata; from the edifying diversions of the popular lecture, the picture gallery, and even the sacred service and sermon of the popular preacher; from the refining comforts of the first-class railway coach and the public restaurant; from the character making labors, disciplines and rewards of every academy, college and even law, medical and divinity school, supported by Southern money and attended by white youth; and from the popular respect paid to those who enjoy these things and withheld from those to whom they are forbidden, these "Negro lawyers, teachers, editors, dentists, doctors and preachers, working in peace and multiplying with the increasing ability of their race to support them," are shut out by rules sustained by State legislation, which refuses to share even the Decalogue on equal terms with the Negro. . . . Where has this New South movement opened to colored people, paying taxes or not, professionally educated or not, the privileges of a single public library?[14]

Unlike *The Grandissimes, Madame Delphine,* and *Dr. Sevier, John March, Southerner* does not clearly condemn the social evils it dramatizes—mob violence, corruption in government, the abridgment of civil rights, the lassitude of religious organizations, the venality of newspaper editors—and it takes no stand on the questions it poses. Its picture of people and events is often acidly realistic, and it invites interpretive comment from an author whose silence seems an abdication of his office.

John March, Southerner is evidence that Cable "was determined to avoid the sort of controversy which had raged about him in the past,"[15] but it is more than that. It is proof that he had abandoned the role of social critic and was relinquishing the debated ground he had once felt duty bound to hold against all challenges. The change is not astonishing. Many a zealous young reformer has turned staunch conservative by middle age; more than one social critic has become a social climber. As Howells remarked in *The Quality of Mercy* (1892), "we are each of us good for only a certain degree of advance in opinion; few men are indefinitely progressive." In *The Grandissimes*, Frowenfeld is told that after he has been in New Orleans a while he will learn to compromise his rigid principles: "the water must expect to take the shape of the bucket." Frowenfeld replies, "One need not be water!" But there is no Frowenfeld in *John March, Southerner*. Cable, after ten years in the North, was finding little difficulty in conforming to the bucket.

CHAPTER *9*

On the Road to Romance

IN THE 1880's Cable was concerned about social problems;
in the 1890's he was involved in the literary dilemma of the
age. The local color vogue had faded, and Cable found himself
faced with the necessity of choosing sides in the battle between
realism and romanticism. The established magazines which had
once set the nation's standards for serious writing—*Century*,
Scribner's, *Harper's*, *Atlantic*—were now purveying unqualified
romance, but newer and bolder journals—*McClure's*, *Munsey's*,
Cosmopolitan—were offering the work of writers who felt that
literature must include aspects of life that were neither picturesque nor genteel. Hamlin Garland, whose fiction Richard
Watson Gilder rejected lest the author's colloquialisms should
corrupt *Century* readers, published *Crumbling Idols* while *John
March, Southerner* was running as a serial. Propounding a
different sort of realism from that which Howells had endorsed
in 1891 in *Criticism and Fiction*, Garland praised vigorous young
writers like E. W. Howe, Henry Blake Fuller, Harold Frederic,
and Stephen Crane.

Cable, who joined Hamilton Wright Mabie and Garland in a
public discussion on "Realism and Romance" in March, 1894,
thought the two techniques not incompatible. His personal
character was compounded of a talent for analytical thought
and a strong taste for sentiment. Romance and realism he had
blended successfully in his early books. He saw, however, that
he could not but be affected by the conflict that was evolving
between what had come to seem opposing literary aesthetics.
Editors and readers called upon him for more picturesque
books with the charm of *Old Creole Days*, but what had been
his private literary domain he must now share with others:
Grace King's *Monsieur Motte* (1888) and *Balcony Stories* (1893)

and Kate Chopin's *Bayou Folks* (1894) were flattering local color pictures of old Louisiana. When Cable turned toward realism, he lost favor with his friends at Century Company. Yet he had outgrown the style of his early fiction, and he could not forego, without further experimentation, the effort to make his writing true to the serious realities of human experience in a specific, clearly delineated environment. His next book, *Strong Hearts*, presents the record of his experimentation before he capitulated, as Hamlin Garland was to do also, to romance.

I *A Variety of Interests*

During the five years that passed between the publication of *John March, Southerner* and the appearance of *Strong Hearts* in 1899, Cable was busy with a variety of interests. There were platform readings, ceremonious plantings of memorial trees on the grounds at "Tarryawhile," appearances as a celebrity at Smith College. Partly as a natural, almost inevitable, response to the needs of the community and partly because of the hard labor and devoted service of Cable and Adelene Moffat, the Home Culture Clubs enjoyed a steady growth. One development that Cable engineered had little to do with adult education or fireside reading clubs for the uncultured masses, though it must have been the expectation that these objectives would be served that led Edward H. R. Lyman to give the money that made possible the expansion of the *Letter*.

That Cable intended to make the little journal something more than a house organ may be seen in his letter of February 25, 1895, to Adelene Moffat, in which he playfully offered a pound of chocolates if she and the staff could make the next issue a six-page publication, without padding. At first, it seems, the journal had been largely Adelene Moffat's responsibility, though Cable read proof, edited the contributions, and wrote for it himself, even when his platform bookings took him away from Northampton. But his personal control became more evident as the evolution progressed.

The issue dated July 1, 1895, featured a new cover designed by Cable's oldest daughter, Louise Cable Chard; once Adelene Moffat's art pupil and later her partner in a studio, she had designed covers for novels in New York. Two numbers later the masthead announced that the journal was edited by Cable, Adelene Moffat, and Emily Dickinson's friend, Mabel Loomis Todd. Mrs. Todd's husband, professor of astronomy at Amherst, had contributed to the previous issue a reading list for beginning students of his subject. A decidedly improved issue in December included poems by Anna Hempstead Branch[1] and Edward D. Merriman; an item on the heavens by a regular contributor, Professor Mary E. Byrd of the Smith College Observatory; increased advertising; and jokes. There were the usual columns reporting on activities of the scattered reading clubs and the classes at the Northampton clubhouse plus an article on readings in Tudor history by Madeleine Wallin.[2] For the first time the cover significantly omitted reference to the Home Culture movement, describing the journal as "devoted to every form of Knowledge, Speculation and Experiment designed to makes homes better homes and neighbors better neighbors."

The January, 1896, number included two poems by Anna Hempstead Branch; a report on club reading by Mary K. Brewster; and an item by Viola Roseboro', the Tennessee writer, who stayed at Adelene Moffat's house for a short while in the spring. She impressed one of Miss Moffat's roomers as "brilliant and entertaining; decidedly unconventional—sitting out on the piazza, day after day, with a man's Derby hat on, or retiring to her room to smoke cigarettes."[3]

Cable's contributions to the expanding journal were now signed and formal and concerned with literature rather than social service. He wrote on Mark Twain for the February issue and on Richard Watson Gilder the next month. For that issue there were contributions from such regulars as Anna Hempstead Branch and Viola Roseboro'. As always, Cable enjoyed the loyal support of his family. Mrs. Louise Cable supplied an article on "Co-operative Cooking" for her department ("Little Chapters on the Kitchen"), and daughter Lucy, writing as "Lucy Leffingwell," contributed a short romantic tale, "The King's Fool and the Sage." Cable evidently did the editorials; Adelene Moffat reported the club news; and Anna Gertrude Brewster, replacing her sister Mary on the staff, wrote an article on suggested readings for the month. Lucy Cable's poem in the April number was accompanied by an illustration by her sister Louise. On the same page began Cable's article on Eugene

Field. Other contributors were Anna Gertrude Brewster, Adelene Moffat, Edwin Oviatt, and Albert Bigelow Paine. Ruth McEnery Stuart, once Cable's fellow worker for the church in New Orleans, was the subject of a profile by Cable and of a letter by Frank R. Stockton. She was also the author of a letter telling Cable he was "not on'y expected but des nachelly requi-ed ter turn up at [New York] on nex' Chuesday evenin'."

Cable wrote on Smith's President Seelye and Hamlin Garland contributed to the May issue of the journal, now described as a monthly aid and guide to reading. In June Mrs. Cable's piece was in praise of a mechanical dishwasher, operated by turning a crank to drench the dishes in the rack with hot soapy water and then to rinse them. Mary E. Burt, close friend of the Cables, had a sentimental sketch on the first page of that number, beneath two poems by Madeleine Wallin. An article on Frederic Remington appeared in July, evidence that the magazine had come to feature art and artists almost as much as literature. The August number printed "Theology," by Paul Laurence Dunbar, the Negro poet whom Cable had met before the notice by Howells in *Harper's Weekly*, June 27, 1896, brought him to national attention. For this ambitious issue and the one in September, which bore little resemblance to the original three-page house organ of four years earlier, Cable conducted a column on literature.

Now Cable thought he saw an opportunity for a career as editor and found the prospect attractive. In October the *Letter* became the *Symposium*, "a monthly literary magazine edited and published by George W. Cable," but listing as its editorial address 41 Gothic Street, the Home Culture building. It was hardly necessary to announce, as Cable did, that the new journal had the same program and was in the same hands as its predecessor, for his "Thoughts and Views" column, Adelene Moffat's "Home and Neighbor," and Anna Gertrude Brewster's "In the Reading World," were obvious transplants from the *Letter*. The first *Symposium* carried other familiar names: Viola Roseboro', Mary E. Burt, Anna Hempstead Branch, and Madeleine Wallin. Another contributor was Mrs. Jennie Weir, Adelene Moffat's sister, who had supplied Cable with notes on Monteagle, Tennessee, when he was writing *John March, Southerner*.

As he had done before, Cable solicited his friends and family for manuscripts and art work. George Henry Clements, the Creole artist who had been his friend for many years, was represented in both the October issue and that for December, in which Helen M. Cox, Cable's niece and once Adelene Moffat's partner in an art studio, had a drawing. In addition to his column, Cable did a major piece for each of the three issues that constituted the magazine's full run. He supplied a second-hand anecdote, "The Brown Ghost," in October; "To See Our Life as Romance Sees It" in November; and "A Visit from Barrie" in December. As his friends had predicted, the response to the new magazine was insufficient to permit its continuance. Cable mourned its demise but was consoled by another opportunity. In February, 1897, he went to New York to assume the editorial management of *Current Literature*.

Although the salary was small and his contract short, he had hoped that the moribund periodical might be made to yield the financial security he sorely needed. He thought, too, that New York's stimulating cultural climate might revive his creative powers. With the April, 1897, issue, when Cable took over as editor, *Current Literature* became a projection of the *Letter* and the *Symposium*. In his editorial columns Cable treated his pet topics—morality in art, the function of dialect, the merits of his literary contemporaries—with competence but no great distinction. Writing under a pseudonym at the editor's insistence, Adelene Moffat contributed a book review and an article on Howard Pyle as an illustrator. Cable once thought of changing the title of the magazine to *Current Literature and Art*. In his series on great editors he included tributes to five of the men who had published his own writing. All of Cable's work as an editor was rooted in the past, though it echoed but faintly the bold cries that came from him in the 1880's.

The titles of the *Letter* and the *Symposium* show how important the Open Letter Club remained in his memory, as does the department in *Current Literature* he called "Editor's Symposium" and described, inaccurately and with a touch of quaintness indicative of its lack of vigor, as "an open tabletalk around the literary board." Whatever success he had in revitalizing the periodical, his dream of a career as its editor did not materialize. He left New York determined to be done with the non-literary activities and "recluse's life" he felt he had fallen into at

Northampton. He wanted, he said, to find something that not only would keep him in the main current of affairs of the world but also would make his life as fruitful—by which he now meant pleasant—as possible.

If he had reached the point where, like the vast majority of mankind, he was unwilling to make consequential sacrifices for worthy causes and was uninterested in working to improve the lot of the underprivileged, he had not lost his taste for the veneration of the public and the respect of the talented, wealthy, or influential men he wanted to regard as his peers. Respect and veneration he must have, for one achievement if not for another. At this stage of his life, having disengaged himself from the race controversy and relinquished the Bible classes, he might have been content to abandon his other non-literary activities—if he had attained eminence as an editor. But he was essentially a gregarious man, a joiner, and one under a compulsion to identify his name with "good works." Once it became necessary for him to return to Northampton, it was imperative that he resume his civic activities there; to have done otherwise would have made him a recluse indeed. In New York he had come to think of his years in Northampton as a retirement, and it was a sharp disappointment to realize he must leave the metropolis and settle again in the hinterland. But Cable was as much drawn to public life as he was to literature, and there were enough advantages to be gained from his principal non-literary interest, the Home Culture Clubs, to warrant—to require —that he continue his commitment to the enterprise.

While he was immersed in his editorial prospects in New York, he could face the possible death of the Home Culture movement without undue concern. A slackening of his devotion to the "dear good work" showed in his attitude toward the crisis that occurred when Adelene Moffat wrote him in April, 1897, that she could not continue as general secretary because the job had exhausted her physical resources and was preventing her from pursuing her work in art, on which she felt she must finally depend for a livelihood. Cable transmitted her resignation to the board of managers and sent also a financial statement which revealed that Miss Moffat was due over fifteen hundred dollars in arrears on her salary. He did not mention that for years the net income from the art work she did at her studio was deducted from the amount due her as wages from the Home Culture Clubs. She was no longer his private secretary, but evidently the provisions he had written into their contract of 1889 were applied after she ceased to be his personal employee. The loss of her services, Cable noted, would probably mean the end of the enterprise.

Though seemingly undisturbed by this possibility, he was relieved when Edward Lyman offered to guarantee half the general secretary's current salary if the balance could be raised by other means. The board, which left direct operations to President Cable, voted to accept Miss Moffat's arrears of salary as a moral obligation to be paid when practicable, but it took no steps to discharge the indebtedness or to correct the slipshod accounting and precarious financing of the work. With some reluctance, Cable agreed to drop the sponsorship of reading clubs—his idea, on founding the movement, of what the Home Culture work should be—and to concentrate on the activities at the local clubhouse. Cable spoke of the spontaneous growth of the work in Northampton, though in reality it was less spontaneous than it was the product of Adelene Moffat's energy and imagination and of her study of the programs of the social service agencies developing throughout the country.

Once stripped of the pseudocultural trappings, the Home Culture Clubs became an agency in which all elements of the little city took justifiable pride. The underprivileged saw it as an opportunity for economic and social advancement; the middle and upper classes, the main source of financial support, recognized its value in providing trained domestic servants (much in demand), an improved labor supply, and Americanization for the large immigrant population. The college girls continued to serve as leaders (teachers) for the individual clubs (classes), but by 1896 twenty per cent of the classes were conducted by Northampton citizens. The agency was an adjunct of the town, not of the college, and the increased participation of townspeople made it possible to extend the program of instruction and to approach one of the theoretical objectives of Cable's original idea: the breaking down of needless class distinctions.

Adelene Moffat submitted her resignation, very probably, with the intent to achieve a curtailment of her duties by ridding the agency of responsibility for the scattered reading clubs and to obtain guarantees that her salary would be paid. Satisfied with the new arrangement, she withdrew the resignation. She did not wish to leave Northampton or to abandon the social work she loved, though it is true that she regarded herself as a professional artist and was concerned about her financial insecurity. For several years she had maintained a studio at Holyoke; but, when she built her own home on Dryads' Green on a lot she bought from Cable, she used the third floor as a studio. At times one or another of the relatives who moved from Tennessee to Northampton lived with her. Like Mary Louise Cable, now located on Elm Street, Miss Moffat provided room and board for Smith College girls and others. For several years Clarence B. Roote, principal of Northampton High School, and his wife lived there. Mrs. Roote was often Miss Moffat's companion at lectures and the theater and helped with arrangements for her informal Sunday night suppers.

Cable's home was the scene of more elaborate social gatherings when the author played host to faculty members of Smith College or to celebrities like A. Conan Doyle and Joseph Jefferson on their professional appearances in Northampton. An event which enhanced Cable's social standing, fed his ego, and led, if only indirectly, to important material benefits, was the visit in October, 1896, of James M. Barrie, who said the attractions he came to the United States to see were George Cable and Niagara Falls. Cable and Barrie, who shared diminutive stature, romantic literary tastes, and an interest in reforming the copyright laws, found one another thoroughly admirable. Like many another "Tarryawhile" guest, Barrie planted a tree in Cable's garden and was induced to speak at Smith. He praised Cable to the students as a great American author, a compliment Cable returned in his writings about his English friend. The Cables entertained Barrie, his wife, and editor W. Robertson Nicoll at a reception that was a memorable evening for the city's elite, though some of them thought the affair was capped by the simple tea Adelene Moffat gave for the notables in her studio the next night.

Barrie urged Cable to visit England, assuring him he could meet expenses by giving readings from his books. When Cable's editorial stint with *Current Literature* came to an end the following year, he turned to Barrie's proposal as one likely to satisfy his wish for a more rewarding life than he had attained in Northampton. In April, 1898, he sailed for England, embarked —alone—on the fruitful life he had promised himself.

No episode in his life was more gratifying than this triumphant first trip abroad. The English, captivated by his personal charm, applauded his drawing room readings from work written decades earlier. Cable's letters to Northampton rang with the names of the authors, officials, lords, and ladies he met. Of lasting importance was his visit to the estate of Andrew Carnegie, whom he had first met through Gilder in 1883. Cable appropriated for his eclectic Home Culture Clubs the idea for the garden competition Carnegie sponsored in Dunfermline. The author's adroit persistence in describing the achievement and the promise of his Northampton agency bore fruit a few years later in a large grant from the philanthropist, and careful cultivation of his acquaintance with the Carnegies finally brought Cable an annuity for his declining years. The trip was an unqualified success. Cable, the ex-reformer, wrote when it was over in July that the world, just as it was, was so good that he could not hope for heaven. For this Christian's Pilgrim's Progress, England had been Vanity Fair.

Cable resumed the pattern of his life in Northampton, but it was months before the glory of his travels wore off. In November he spoke to the Northampton Social and Literary Club about his impressions of England. He was away on a reading tour in January, 1899, when the death of Edward Lyman, chief patron of the Home Culture Clubs, posed a new threat to that agency. Cable and Adelene Moffat resolved that the work somehow must go on, but it was Frank Lyman, Miss Moffat's friend, who saved the enterprise with the announcement that the family expected to continue the support his late father and mother had always given it. He and his sister made the agency an outright gift of the premises on Center Street. In May, when Lyman was elected to fill his father's place on the board of managers, the agency seemed to rest on as firm a foundation as it had ever enjoyed. Cable's personal economic position improved somewhat with the publication of *Strong Hearts*. He wrote Adelene Moffat jubilantly in September that his works (which Scribner's made available in a variety of reissues and new editions) were selling better than usual and that the first issue of his new book was sold out.

II   *Strong Hearts*

Strong Hearts is composed of two stories and a novella which are unrelated except for the appearance of Richard Thorndyke Smith and a Louisiana setting in each. "The Taxidermist," published in *Scribner's Magazine* in May, 1893, is preceded in the book by "The Solitary," which was called "Gregory's Island" when it came out in *Scribner's* in August, 1896, and is followed by the novella, "The Entomologist," which the magazine ran in three installments beginning in January, 1899. In preparing the narratives for book publication, Cable added a few scattered lines and an introductory chapter in which he insisted that the three stories are one because they illustrate "the indivisible twinship of Poetry and Religion."

"The Taxidermist" tells of a Creole, "Pas-Trop-Bon" Manouvrier, who wins $75,000 in the lottery. He and his wife use the money to build a fine house but delay moving into it because they are reluctant to alter their humble, idyllic way of life. When fire destroys a nearby orphanage, the childless Manouvriers turn their new home over to the children and thank God for the babies the lottery has brought them. This traditional, unimportant tale helps plot Cable's course of development. Careful to avoid controversy, he refrains from any suggestion of a slur on the Creoles and even brings himself to praise their ancestry. A crass American serves as contrast for the sensitive taxidermist, who is so admirable a man that the narrator, Smith, ponders "the fineness of soul and life" that "existed in earlier generations" to produce him. Moreover, the lottery that Cable had assailed in the *Picayune* in 1872 and used as antagonist in " 'Sieur George" is now portrayed as an agent of accidental benevolence. When one character speaks of it as a "hideous canker poisoning the character and blasting the lives of every class of our people," Smith assents absently and walks away, ashamed of himself because "a man without a quick, strong, aggressive, insistent indignation against undoubted evil is a very poor stick." Cable was willing to use the lottery to make a story; he was now unwilling to write a story to attack an "undoubted evil." It was better to be a poor stick than a scorned reformer.

The first of the three narratives in *Strong Hearts* (but the second in order of composition), "The Solitary" moves away from local color and is basically unlike anything else Cable wrote. Customarily Cable's narratives feature a man *versus* man conflict in the main plot, with a man *versus* society conflict, centered on the minor characters, emerging as the real subject. "The Solitary," however, is concerned with man against himself and with man against nature—conflicts Cable had disregarded in the past. Furthermore, it has an internal angle of narration and a psychological, rather than a sociological, emphasis. Cable had treated drunkards before, but Gregory, the solitary, is the first evidence that he understood something of the nature of alcoholism and could deal with it objectively and sympathetically. Howells, of course, had done this with a minor character in *The Lady of the Aroostock* (1879); S. Weir Mitchell was to do it even better in *Circumstance* (1901). But neither of these novelists complicated his picture of a man's struggles to overcome his compulsions by placing the character's life in danger in a hostile physical environment.

The narrator, who was simply a Mr. Smith connected with the fire insurance business in "The Taxidermist," has now become Richard Thorndyke Smith, engaged in banking as well as insurance and sharing with Cable an addiction to sentimentality and superficial moralizing. Smith had met Gregory when both were Confederate soldiers and when Gregory was beginning to fear "a drunkard's life and a drunkard's death." After the war Smith marries, but Gregory, a rejected lover, remains a bachelor. Gregory operates a small schooner on Mississippi Sound, but drinking makes him a failure in business. Fear of his compulsion, rather than courage, drives him to a desperate act. He takes a small boat out on the Gulf, lands on a deserted little island, smashes the boat, and waits to ride out his overpowering temptation. Finally his thirst masters him. He builds a raft with which to return to the mainland but is saved from himself when a hurricane smashes his makeshift craft. By the time the steamer arrives to rescue him from his prison, he has regained control of himself. Aware that he will again submit to temptation if he is where he can do so, Gregory settles on the island, though it is dangerously exposed and likely to be submerged at any moment,[4] becomes a cattle raiser there, and attains the inevitable material rewards poetic justice demands. The O. Henry ending —the revelation that Gregory was once Mrs. Smith's suitor—is only a minor blemish, since it is decorative rather than structural. Cable's wild setting, remote from the populous streets and quaint buildings of Creole New Orleans, is described with an attention to detail and a controlled poetic imagination that make it vividly exciting. Had he dispensed with the smug moralizing of Richard Thorndyke Smith, he would have had a story worthy of comparison with "The Open Boat," which Stephen Crane published a year after Cable's tale was first printed.

"The Entomologist" was written while Cable was in New York editing *Current Literature* and at a time when he was studying the literary figures and movements of the day. His editorial comments do not show profound knowledge of the works of Henry James, but they do establish Cable's general acquaintance with the style of a man he seemingly admired as an author and, in general, respected as a person. The two men had met in New York in 1883; they had spent some time together when Cable was in England in 1898; and they saw one another again when James visited Northampton in 1906. James had been there before, in 1864, as a young man, resting and taking the famous water cure. He used the town as the scene of his first important novel, *Roderick Hudson* (1876). Roderick Hudson's talent was not appreciated in Northampton, which found his sculpture shocking. What chance, James asked, had a man of genius to fulfill himself in so provincial an American town as Northampton? Cable was asking himself the same question when he was at work on "The Entomologist" in 1897 and was hoping his genius would be saved by an editorial career in New York. Both the matter and the manner of that story may be attributed to the influence of Henry James, whether or not Cable was consciously aware of the indebtedness.

Set against the background of the yellow fever epidemic of 1878, "The Entomologist" is a tale of domestic entanglement told by a narrator who is rather the moralizing observer than the central consciousness of the sort James employed, though the story has a decidedly Jamesian flavor. Richard Thorndyke-

Smith watches an affair develop between the New England wife of his Creole friend and a German entomologist, a gross man uninterested in women but so lacking in a moral sense that he is led, "bit by bit, down the precipitous incline between her vaporous refinements and his wallowing animalisms." His own devoted wife resolutely refuses to be disturbed by her husband's impending fall: "I sink sare will be not storm if sare iss no sunder," she says. Fontenette, the jealous Creole husband, manfully contains his anger. Yellow fever strikes before the illicit affair can reach a serious stage; the crime is one of intent, not of commission. Mrs. Fontenette redeems herself by heroic nursing and by demonstrating her love for her husband before she dies. The Baron, untroubled by serious qualms of conscience for his "first steps in perfidy," is a victim of his physical appetites; he dies of injudicious eating while he is recovering from the fever. "So they both, caterpillar and rose, were gone." After a few years pass, the noble German widow, discovered to be a countess, marries Fontenette. This seems an epilogue to allow Cable to provide for this novella the culminating love interest Richard Watson Gilder had withheld from *Dr. Sevier* by insisting that widowed Mary Richling must not become the wife of the physician.

At the outset, "The Entomologist" promises to be a penetrating study of marital infidelity, a parallel to *The Awakening*, the strong novel about mixed marriage and adultery that Kate Chopin published in the same year. But Cable's tale becomes melodrama when the epidemic strikes and is banal magazine romance at the close. The bold subject is first weakened by his mannered style and then obscured as his attention moves to the terrors of the yellow fever; his descriptions echo the letters about his own experiences which he had sent to Boyesen and Gilder more than twenty years earlier. The shift in emphasis weakens the story structure since it forces the resolution to depend on the epidemic, not on the characters. The theme—the superiority of feeling to intellect, of morality to science—is sounded in all Cable's non-fiction in the closing years of the 1890's. Avoiding further attempts at psychological realism, he openly embraced the precepts of romance.

This development is symbolized in Richard Thorndyke Smith, whose emergence as Cable's alter ego may be traced readily in *Strong Hearts*. In "The Taxidermist" he is simply "Mr. Smith."

Like Cable, he was born in 1844, but he lives on Sixth Street rather than on Eighth. Smith sits at a "counting-desk," as Cable had done for years; but he is an executive of a fire insurance company, a more exalted business position than Cable had held. In "The Solitary," set at an earlier time than "The Taxidermist," Smith becomes Richard Thorndyke Smith, a Confederate veteran residing in New Orleans with his Southern wife. In the chapter Cable added to the story for its publication in the book, Smith is described as being in the business "of banking and finance." His occupation is not mentioned specifically in "The Entomologist," where it is his moral nature that is stressed, but he seems enough a pillar of the community to justify the hyphenated "Thorndyke-Smith" that Mrs. Fontenette assigns to him. This form of the name is used on occasion in the other narratives and essays in which he appears or is referred to. However the details of his personality, age, occupation, etc., may vary, he is invariably an idealization of the author himself. It is significant that Smith has always a more elevated status than Cable had attained at a comparable stage of life.

In February, 1896, Cable gave a series of lectures at Boston's Lowell Institute on "The Story-Teller and His Art," from which he culled material for the journals he was editing and for several vaporous essays on art and morality, imagination and beauty; four of these are organized as dialogues between the author and his New Orleans counterpart.[5] In them Cable makes much ado about his role as squire of "Tarryawhile" and sage of Paradise Woods. Smith is sometimes used as counterpoise to Cable, but generally the two are posturing, pretentious figures so alike that they blend into a single composite. Neither social critic nor reformer, Smith stands for no causes except art and beauty and truth, qualities Cable saw at this time in *The Rubáiyát* and in the works of Hall Caine, Stevenson, Thoreau, Whitman, and Conan Doyle. In his first Civil War romance, *The Cavalier*, Dick Smith is the secondary leading man, a dashing military hero. He is mentioned in *Kincaid's Battery*, which failed to duplicate the meretricious popularity of its predecessor, and in later books. The de-emphasis of Smith in these shows that an era, in which Cable courted regionalism and psychological realism but fell victim to the blandishments of romanticism, had come to an end.

CHAPTER 10

Richard Thorndyke Smith

I *The Cavalier*

CABLE was at work on *The Cavalier* at least as early as 1896, when he made indirect reference to the heroine, Charlotte Oliver, in "Gregory's Island." When the novel was completed in April, 1900, it proved to be a perfect embodiment of the convenient literary standards he had been evolving over the last six years. Rejected by several magazine editors, it was published without serialization in 1901, when it won a popular success unparalleled by any of Cable's other books. He did not profess that *The Cavalier* treated the past with historical accuracy, but he claimed that the book preserved its spirit. Actually the novel ignores the issues of the Civil War and the contentious spirit of that heroic era in favor of concentration on a love affair. The sale of a hundred thousand copies by the end of the year proved that the author had judged the taste of the reading public correctly.

It was not in his literary aesthetic alone that Cable continued to move toward conformity with the dominant spirit of the times. From an orthodoxy verging on sanctimony, his personal creed had developed along latitudinarian lines; his religion was now a loose and comfortable garment. His appearances on the platform, less numerous than in the past, were confined to routine readings from his works. Rarely did he speak on the race question, as he did to a society of colored people in Boston in November, 1901. Evidently he touched on the old controversy when he led discussions of Northampton's Social and Literary Club in February, 1900, and April, 1903; but the talk "The Relation of the Novel and the Drama," which he gave to his fellow "apostles" in February, 1902, was more characteristic of his interests and affairs at this time.

His ambition to have his works enacted on the stage, which
had provoked unsuccessful attempts to dramatize the *Bonaventure*
stories and some of the Creole tales, was realized in December,
1902, when Julia Marlowe appeared in *The Cavalier*. Cable had
a part in preparing the novel for the stage and was exultant
when it reached Broadway, but it found too little favor with
critics and audiences to enjoy a long run. For almost twenty
years more, Cable hoped to see stage or movie versions of his
fiction. *The Cavalier* proved to be his nearest approach to
success in what the former puritan liked to call his "theatre
business." The "Julia Marlowe Edition" of the novel, an effort
to capitalize on the dramatization, was issued in 1903. For this
Cable supplied a preface in which he pretends that R. Thorndyke
Smith, banker and underwriter, who prefers to be called a
"memorist" instead of a novelist because he writes of true events,
is really the author. The statement seems less a pose than a
profound truth uttered in jest. *The Cavalier* has so few of the
qualities that distinguish Cable's best fiction as to seem, indeed,
the product of some other pen than his own.

The narrator of the swashbuckling romance is Richard
Thorndyke Smith, a slight Confederate cavalryman of nineteen.
Smith and the hero, Ned Ferry, take part in sorties and skirmishes
a-plenty;[1] but, for all that these encounters have to do with
the issues of the Civil War, they might have been set in the
Ruritania that Anthony Hope conceived in 1894 for his *Prisoner
of Zenda* rather than in Mississippi. Because the book is less a
"history . . . of war than of love," the battles are important
only as they determine whether Lieutenant Ferry and the
glamorous Confederate spy, Charlotte Oliver, will "make life's
long march in sunshine together or in darkness apart." Little
concerned with character development, Cable weaves a complex
fabric of intrigue, half-truths, hints, dreams, and double-dealing.
At one point Smith sums up the situation thus:

> Ned Ferry, loving Charlotte Oliver, yet coerced by his sense
> of a soldier's duty, had put passion's dictates wholly aside and
> had set about to bring these murderers [Charlotte's husband and
> father-in-law] to justice; doing this though he knew that she
> could never with honor or happiness to either of them become
> the wife of a man who had made her a widow, while she,
> aware of his love, a love so true that he would not breathe it

to her while this hideous marriage held her, had ridden perilously in the dead of night to circumvent his plans if, with honor to both of them, it could be done.

Theatrical heroics, in "the dead of night" and otherwise, are performed by "Federals" and Confederates alike. Gallantry and nobility are assigned generously and impartially to civilians and to soldiers in blue and in grey. The sentimental melodrama is epitomized in one scene, a troublesome climax in the stage adaptation, in which Charlotte sings "The Star Spangled Banner" at the bedside of a dying Union officer.

Though he models his young narrator on himself, Cable endows other figures with some of the traits that had characterized him as a youth, and he makes the hero, Ferry, representative of the values to which he presently subscribed. One sanctimonious soldier, Scott Gholson, is just such a "religionist" as Cable had been as a cavalry recruit; Ferry, who reads Voltaire and George Sand and questions the Bible, is the "romanticist" Cable had become. Ferry drinks and plays cards and dances and holds as his religion no more sectarian dogma than the belief that "there's something right about everything that's beautiful and something wrong about everything that isn't." Like Ferry, Smith is entranced by worldly Charlotte, and his love affair with the younger Camille Harper is touched with delicate sensuality. Sensuality is inherent to the situation which lies at the heart of the plot: Charlotte's unconsummated marriage to a scoundrel who appears in scenes notable for their sordid realism. The smattering of Creole dialect, the glimpses of social reality, the skillful delineation of minor characters—Cable's hallmarks—are incidental to his absorption in sentiment and cloak-and-dagger intrigue. There is more of the same in *Kincaid's Battery*, a second Civil War romance, on which Cable was at work by the end of 1902.

II *Bylow Hill*

In March, 1902, installments of *Bylow Hill* began to appear in *Atlantic Monthly*. The last of Cable's novels to make its debut in a magazine, *Bylow Hill* is his only long fiction restricted to a Northern scene. He made few changes in the true story, given him by Dr. S. Weir Mitchell, on which he based this short, undistinguished book. Again the antagonist is a minister—though one whose villainy may be excused by his derangement—and again the plot involves a mismatched couple and marital infidelity. Arthur Winslow, a neurotic clergyman, is insanely and unjustifiably suspicious of his wife's relationship with her former fiancé, Leonard Byington. On his knees he cries, "Oh, my wife, my wife! save me, save me! Hell is in my soul!" The intolerable situation is resolved when the crazed husband plunges to his death as he flees in terror from the wife he has dreamed he killed. Released from her martyrdom, his widow finds happiness in marriage to Byington.

Cable's early Creole fiction treats marriage, in itself a happy ending, as a sacred institution and an ideal state, but in *John March, Southerner,* "The Entomologist," *The Cavalier,* and *Bylow Hill*—all written after the birth of his last child and before the death of his first wife—there are incompatible couples and instances of real or suspected infidelity. The change in Cable's attitude toward matrimony may not seem significant, but it should not be disregarded.

Certainly *Bylow Hill* is Cable's poorest novel. Driven by his interest in the theater, he made the book little more than a series of scenes (though some of the most crucial action takes place "off stage" and is reported by letter), with the narrative development and characterization largely dependent on dialogue. The opening chapter presents six major characters, not one shown in any depth. Some of them speak "a delicious Southern accent," but their words are given in conventional form, "as they thought they spoke them." There is much Irish brogue and some rustic dialogue, but the speech and the speakers come from the stage, not from life.

Three explanations for the weaknesses of the book may be offered. The first is Cable's failure to heed S. Weir Mitchell's warning about the difficulties involved in attempting the story without a proper knowledge of insanity. Cable had opportunity to study mental illness as both a medical and a social problem. Dr. Edward B. Nimms, superintendent of Northampton State Hospital, an institution for the insane, was a fellow member of the Northampton Social and Literary Club and one of the original supporters of the Home Culture Clubs. Cable also knew his successor, Dr. John A. Houston, a later member of the agency's board. Despite these opportunities, Cable chose to regard Arthur Winslow's condition from a superficial moral point of view and to exploit it for its dramatic possibilities. In the second place, forgetting that his strongest characters are those who personify a specific culture which is itself his real subject, he neglected to integrate his setting, characters, and action. Long a resident of Massachusetts, he was as qualified to write about a New England town as Mark Twain was to depict a Hartford mechanic in King Arthur's Camelot, but Cable gave his setting no organic function. Finally, because he lacked a facile imagination, Cable needed memories of his own experiences and careful observation of models to give depth and vitality to his artistic creations. Without these aids he could not construct an effective novel from a borrowed true story, whatever that story's inherent values might be.

III *A People's College*

For years Cable's ambition, as he wrote Adelene Moffat in January, 1891, had been to get his fireside reading clubs securely established and able to maintain themselves without his active direction. Now that the reading clubs had given way to community service and adult education at the Northampton clubhouse, his sights shifted to a more elevated target. It was probably about the time *Bylow Hill* appeared in book form that Cable, president of the Home Culture Clubs, began seriously to envision himself as founder of a people's college.

All about him in the Northampton area were colleges (notably Smith, Amherst, and Mount Holyoke) and similar institutions (such as Clarke School for the Deaf, Burnham School for Girls, and Williston Seminary), all of them serving as living memorials to the foresight and public spirit of their founders. Many of his associates were college professors and administrators, and even the businessmen in his circle shared the general interest in what was one of the community's major commodities—education. All across the country, philanthropists were establishing colleges: Vanderbilt (1873), Johns Hopkins (1876), Leland Stanford (1885), the University of Chicago (1892). On his reading tours Cable had become acquainted with many of the nation's educational institutions; he had seen some of them grow from humble beginnings to positions of honor and influence within a relatively short time.

While his national reputation as an author was important to his status in Northampton when he first settled there, it had come to be overshadowed locally by his civic activities, ranging from brief talks at programs of the Northampton Debating Society to the management of the Home Culture Clubs, an enterprise the community thoroughly approved. No significant expansion of the educational program of that agency could be made without an enlarged physical plant. In 1902 Cable arranged with the school board to use the Center Street Grammar School as an annex at night;[2] but local resources, heavily burdened by the needs of Northampton's exceptionally numerous charities, could do little more to improve the Home Culture Clubs' physical facilities. He must look for funds elsewhere.

Cable's first appeal for funds from Andrew Carnegie was rejected on January 16, 1900, on the ground that the philanthropist was interested only in libraries. After he succeeded in obtaining money from Carnegie to support the annual flower-garden competition, Cable decided to approach him again. He broached his new request to Mrs. Carnegie, but it was some time before he reached her husband with his appeal. In February, 1903, a few days after the receipt of a gift of $500 from Mrs. Arthur Curtis James to extend the program of instruction in household arts, Carnegie agreed to contribute $50,000 for buildings, the same amount he had decided to grant to Mount Holyoke College in December.[3] In his anxiety to prevent public knowledge of the planned expansion from affecting real estate values, Cable waited until April to mention the gift to Adelene Moffat, who was abroad for a year of art study. After a tract of land adjacent to the Center Street clubhouse was bought, plans were drawn to remodel its frame mansion, the Boise homestead (which became "James House"), and to erect a new headquarters building, "Carnegie House." On her return to Northampton in August, Adelene Moffat joined Cable in soliciting the increased local financial support needed to meet the proviso with which Carnegie qualified his gift.

In January, 1904, Cable wrote from his wife's bedside in New York to send Miss Moffat instructions about the agency's work. The letters closed with postscript reports on Mrs. Cable's condition. His wife's poor health had been a matter of concern for years. She had been his companion, guide, and assistant during the golden years of his literary and civic life, and she had borne his eight children. The shock of her death in February interrupted his work on *Kincaid's Battery* but had little effect on his energetic planning for the new facilities and expanded program of the Home Culture Clubs.

Calvin Coolidge, then a Northampton lawyer who became a member of the busy board of managers that spring, helped in the selection of the enlarged staff that would be required to operate the agency's new plant. The most important addition was Harry B. Taplin, brought from Boston's South End House early in 1904 as secretary for men's work. Taplin found that Adelene Moffat, demoted from general secretary to secretary for women's work, was "a gifted woman, greatly loved by rich and poor." He soon recognized that Cable and Miss Moffat were "sincerely interested in helping people, but their approach was different—he worked *for* people and she *with* people."[4]

It was Taplin who was assigned to escort the Carnegies on the train from Springfield when they visited Northampton for the dedication of "Carnegie House" on April 12, 1905. Northampton exerted itself to honor the philanthropist. Cable and Carnegie spoke briefly at Smith College and again at an evening program at the Academy of Music. Cable praised all the agency's sponsors, lauded Carnegie, and congratulated the five hundred club members who were present: "your People's College is proud of you."[5] He did not once mention Adelene Moffat, who sat in the audience with the staff members.

A month later, Cable sailed for England, this time accompanied by his daughter Lucy. The trip was a holiday, not a triumphal tour. He gave no readings but did repeat one of the highlights of his earlier visit when he and Lucy spent a week with the Carnegies at Skibo Castle in Scotland. On his return to Northampton in July, he resumed work on *Kincaid's Battery* and participation in the civic affairs of the community. He had hardly unpacked before he suggested that the authorities at Williston Seminary invite Harry Taplin there to give a series of lectures on labor problems like those he had offered at Smith and Amherst, but Williston had no funds for the purpose.

Taplin resigned to take an attractive position in Boston just as the Home Culture season was about to get underway in September, 1906. His replacement, Herbert D. Hemenway, had no professional training or experience in social work but compensated for this, in Cable's eyes, by his knowledge of horticulture and his ability to promote the annual flower-garden competition, the Home Culture project in which Cable took the greatest personal interest.[6]

In November, Cable married Eva C. Stevenson, whom he had met in Kentucky five years earlier. His children, most of them married now and living away from Northampton, welcomed "Aunt Eva" into the family, and she assumed an active role in his public affairs. Adelene Moffat was co-hostess for a "large and brilliant reception" in honor of Cable and his new wife.[7] An accomplished woman, the new Mrs. Cable brought to "Tarryawhile" pictures, marbles, bronzes, and other choice souvenirs of her wide travels and made the rather bare house a home again.

IV   *A Controversy*

This second marriage, at sixty-two, eased Cable's loneliness and contributed to some renewal of his literary productivity, but it may also have provoked an incident that mars both his public and private record. In March, 1907, Cable dismissed Adelene Moffat from her post with the Home Culture Clubs, stating on the one hand that expenses necessitated a reduction in the staff and, on the other, that the expanded program required at its head a man, whose function would be like that of a male president of a coeducational college. Miss Moffat was stunned; her friends—rich and poor alike—rose in protest. Newspapers hinted at the gossip that was circulating about the real reason for the sudden dismissal, which was announced to the public as a "resignation." The board of managers approved Cable's autocratic act, though Frank Lyman, still the principal local supporter of the agency, resigned in protest. Other resignations followed in the next few years. Cable's wife and his sister Mary Louise became dominant in the Women's Council, which was reorganized in the wake of its rebellion against the decision of the board.

It was inexpedient of Cable to fire Miss Moffat if he hoped

thereby to put an end to the rumors, for the injustice of the act helped to keep the gossip in circulation. It was being said in Northampton that his marriage to Eva Stevenson had come as a shock to three women, each of whom, it was alleged, Cable had promised to marry in case his first wife should die. After he dismissed Adelene Moffat, not before, Cable heard that she had slandered his first wife, and he wrote to Harry Taplin in Boston for confirmation. Taplin, to whom it was reported that Miss Moffat's remarks had been made, replied indignantly: "How the story may have started I have no idea, but it certainly bears no resemblance to fact, and is surely most unfortunate." He pointed out that certain details of the story Cable had heard made it "without point or meaning and absurd on its very face." Adelene Moffat had made no derogatory remarks to him about Mrs. Louise Cable: "On the contrary I have heard her speak most highly of the former Mrs. Cable," he said.[8]

But Cable evidently chose to believe what he had heard and persuaded his family to do likewise. Except for what she told the Lymans and her lawyer, Miss Moffat said nothing against Cable or the management of the agency for which she had worked nearly twenty years, but evidently Cable was impelled to circulate his side of the controversy rather widely. On April 21 he paid a long call on Mary K. Brewster, who had worked with him and Adelene Moffat on the staff of the *Letter,* and gave her, she reported in her diary, an "intimate detailed relation of the trouble between himself & Miss M." Mary Brewster heard "more discussion of the Cable-Moffat matter" later from other people. It was, as she said, unfortunate.

Newspaper hints of financial irregularities and autocratic management led to two audits (Cable himself had kept the books), a committee investigation, and a general reorganization of the agency over the next few years. Public support declined drastically and the scope of the program was reduced. Part of this curtailment was necessitated by a matter that never came to public attention—Miss Moffat's claims for one thousand dollars in accumulated salary arrears. Attorney John C. Hammond, who had resigned from the board of managers, pressed Miss Moffat's case until it was settled in June, 1908; the board had ignored her claim until that was no longer possible and then it had commissioned Calvin Coolidge to try to arrange a compromise at a reduced figure. The money was raised by mortgaging "Lyman House," the old Center Street building, which was sold outright three years later to put an end to the borrowing that followed Miss Moffat's dismissal. Cable continued to head the agency, which was renamed The People's Institute in 1909, until his retirement in 1920.

Despite Cable's direct effort to prevent her from obtaining the position, Adelene Moffat went to Boston as manager of a group of charities supported by Mrs. Pauline A. (Quincy Agazziz) Shaw. Miss Moffat was an active social worker and professional artist for nearly half a century after she left Northampton. Chagrined as she was by the abrupt termination of her long service to the Home Culture Clubs, she could say without rancor after revisiting the city in 1951: "I have seen a goodish part of the world; east and west, north and south: from the Orient to Iceland and I can honestly say that I have never seen any people anywhere whom I have thought finer than the people of Northampton."[9]

V *Kincaid's Battery*

Cable's literary career was resumed with the publication of *Kincaid's Battery*, in November, 1908, a few months after he was severely jolted by the death of his son William. Conceived as a play, it was written as a novel only after the scenario was rejected. That this is another "history of hearts" is made clear in the opening sentence: "For the scene of this narrative please take into mind a wide quarter-circle of country, such as any of the pretty women we are to know in it might have covered on the map with her half-opened fan." Actually, most of the story takes place in New Orleans, and nothing like a battle occurs until almost midway in the novel; for battle scenes, Cable knew, are difficult to present on the stage.

Although the details of his scene—many derived from his own experiences, some from Mrs. Dora Richards Miller's diary—are as accurate as ever, Cable's wartime New Orleans is hardly more real than the old Creole Louisiana of Victor Herbert's *Naughty Marietta*. He makes little of the opportunity to describe the Crescent City's trials at the hands of General Butler, and again he ignores the underlying issues of the war. The war is a vague background for the love affair of Hillary Kincaid, the artillery captain who has to live down his reputation as a "ladies' man," and Anna Callender, the conventional heroine. The plot hinges on undelivered letters, sliding panels, transparent disguises, and Machiavellian scheming. The snatches of song scattered throughout the book remind one of Cable's practice of closing his platform readings—now at an end—with Creole melodies, and they contribute to the light-opera flavor that permeates every scene.

Just as Howells had used Bartley Hubbard and Basil March in several different books, Cable tries to give his novel body by making allusions to characters in his other works: Ned Ferry, Fontenette, the Grandissimes, Richard Thorndyke Smith, Raoul Innerarity, and Jules St.-Ange. Dr. Sevier makes many appearances as friend and adviser to Anna Callender, as though Cable wished at last to establish the physician's loyalty to the Confederate cause. In later books Cable continued the practice of referring to characters in his former works, less an effort to create a saga than an attempt to benefit from his established reputation.

Scribner's brought out a slender volume in 1909, *"Posson Jone'"* *and Père Raphaël*, composed of two stories that Cable insisted were really one. The former tale had appeared in print in 1876, and the latter, a sequel which Gilder said had the charm of Cable's earliest work, was first published in *Century Magazine* in August, 1901. Edmund Wilson, a more discerning critic than Gilder, describes "Père Raphaël" as "an arid little horror of forced contrivance."[10] It is a characteristic product of Cable's period of pure romance, the nadir that might be called the "Richard Thorndyke Smith Years."

CHAPTER 11

Lover of Louisiana

CABLE hardly finished one book before he began the next, for his account with Scribner's was always overdrawn; and he continued his social and civic interests as far as his age and circumstances would permit. He was one of the founders of the Northampton Historical Society in September, 1905, almost thirty years after he had joined with others in incorporating the Louisiana Historical Society. He was still a joiner; in May, 1909, his application for admission to Northampton's Seth Pomeroy Chapter of the Sons of the American Revolution was accepted. Other interests included the American Academy of Arts and Letters, to which he was elected in 1908; the Simplified Spelling Board; The People's Institute, especially its garden competition; the Northampton Social and Literary Club; Williston Seminary; and Okolona Industrial College, a Negro school in Mississippi.

His efforts, as late as 1907, to help the Okolona president raise money for the institution demonstrate that, while he was no longer a leader in the movement to gain civil rights for the Negro, he had not surrendered his conviction that the nation must extend to all its people—especially those most circumscribed in their opportunities—full participation in the responsibilities and rights of democratic citizenship.[1] Now the Negro cause had a new generation of spokesmen—Oswald Garrison Villard, W. E. B. DuBois, John Haynes Holmes, Charles Edward Russell, Mary White Ovington, and others—and Cable was not one of those who signed the call for the meeting of liberals in New York in 1909 which led to the formation of the National Association for the Advancement of Colored People. William Dean Howells was a signer, and Adelene Moffat spoke at the association's third annual conference in 1913.

Late that year Cable had an operation to remove a cataract

from his eye. The $7,500 Scribner's had advanced on his next novel was spent; it was money from Andrew Carnegie that helped him pay the surgeon's bill and save his home. "Tarryawhile" was no longer the family center, for the children had scattered from Northampton, and even Cable and his wife no longer spent the winters there. Scribner's tried to ease his straitened financial circumstances by collecting in October, 1914, in *The Amateur Garden* the essays on gardening Cable had written for various magazines for ten years. Cable celebrated his seventieth birthday on the twelfth of that month.

I *Gideon's Band*

Like Henry James, Cable was reluctant to recognize that his talent was not for the theater. *Gideon's Band*, the novel he published in September, 1914, records his affectionate admiration for actors and his persistent hope to write a book that might be dramatized. A tale of the Mississippi in the days when his father had dreamed of making his fortune on the river, *Gideon's Band* is sentimental and theatrical, but it marks the beginning of Cable's final literary period. Too much like Edna Ferber's *Show Boat* and too little like Mark Twain's *Life on the Mississippi*, it has, nevertheless, more merit than any book Cable had produced in the twenty years since the publication of *John March, Southerner*.

The story takes place aboard a magnificent side-wheeler making her maiden voyage up the river from New Orleans in 1852. The Hayles and the Courteneys operate rival fleets of steamboats, and both Hayles and Courteneys in abundance are aboard the Courteney's *Votaress*. Asiatic cholera breaks out among the two or three hundred immigrants crowded on the lower deck, and it spreads to some of the cabin passengers. Gideon Hayle's Creole wife nurses the immigrants without regard for her own safety. Her tempestuous twin sons are the provocative agents whose hatred for the Courteneys constitutes the force that must be circumvented before the happy ending can be reached. Hugh Courteney and Ramsey Hayle are hero and heroine: Hugh a stocky, self-contained young man learning to be a Mississippi pilot; Ramsey a scatter-brained fifteen year-old who matures rapidly during the course of the voyage.

Central to the theme of the novel, as was the tale of Bras-Coupé in *The Grandissimes*, is the story of a glamorous quadroon slave, Phyllis, who is the cause of the enmity the Hayles hold for the Courteneys. Phyllis, once the mistress of one of the Hayles, persecuted Hugh Courteney as a child, taking out on the boy, as Cornelius Leggett once did on young John March, her hatred of slavery and of all white people. It was she who accidentally caused the burning of the *Quakeress*, in which disaster, it was supposed, she lost her life some years ago. Phyllis was saved, however, by the Gilmores, a pair of actors who are abolitionists at heart, and she is with them aboard the *Votaress*. A veil conceals her identity—and her striking resemblance to Ramsey Hayle—for a time; its removal adds fuel to the Hayle-Courteney feud. Eight years later, when she has been given her freedom, Phyllis is a chambermaid aboard the *Enchantress*, on which the main characters of *Gideon's Band* are reassembled for the novel's climax. The suicide of the Hale twins, accomplished with the unintentional assistance of Phyllis, makes possible the marriage of Hugh Courteney and Ramsey. But there is no similar happy ending for Phyllis. Cable dooms her to a life of servitude and single blessedness.

Song-laden and contrived though it is, *Gideon's Band* is a sturdy work, not a delicate romance. Cable's descriptions of the steamboat and the exciting river it navigates ring with authenticity. He marshals a multitude of details to create a vivid panorama of the Mississippi in the days of its glory. Much as he is interested in what transpires on the *Votaress*, he often directs attention to the great river itself and to the country through which it passes. All the character types of the Mississippi region are to be found among the passengers on the steamboat. Once again Cable is social critic as well as storyteller.

It is the total culture, presented in microcosm, with which Cable is concerned and on which he comments directly. For example, he says that Basil Hayle, the younger brother of the twins, is the spiritual image of his fellows: "their unqualified straight-forwardness, their complacent rusticity, their childish notions of the uses of wealth, their personal modesty and communal vanity, their happy oblivion to world standards, their extravagance of speech, their political bigotry, their magisterial downrightness, their inflammability, and their fine self-reliance."

The Gilmores encounter other representatives of the culture, a young couple about to go ashore at New Carthage, "a city of seven houses."

> They and the Gilmores sat down at the forward edge of the texas roof, the players finding the Carthaginians very attractive: fluent on morals, cuisine, manners, steamboats, the turf, fashions, the chase; voluble on the burdensomeness of the slave to his master, the blessedness of the master to his slave; but sore to the touch on politics and religion—with their religion quite innocently adjusted to their politics—and promptly going aground on any allusion to history, travel, the poets, statistics, architecture, ornithology, art, music, myths, memoirs, Europe, Asia, Africa, homœopathy or phrenology. It entertained the players just to see how many things the happy lovers knew nothing about and to hear them state in some new form each time they backed off a sand bar of their own ignorance, that they had seen the world, sucked the orange, yet found no spot of earth so perfect to live in as New Carthage.

Among the other passengers are a Methodist bishop and a backwoods Baptist exhorter. The hypocritical bishop is shamed into visiting the sick immigrants and pays with his life; the bigoted exhorter is castigated throughout the book. What a transformation! Cable—ex-Sabbatarian, deacon of Edwards Congregational Church, father-in-law of a clergyman—makes his ministers ignoble and shamelessly idealizes a pair of actors!

If in this book Cable shows little disposition to apply his social criticism to any problems more contemporary or specific than parochialism and hypocrisy, he uses it at least to reassert the condemnation of slavery—as moral wickedness, economic stupidity, and political villainy—which he had included in his first novel thirty-five years earlier. One agent for this attack on the South's cherished institution is Joy, Ramsey's black nurse. Less outspoken than Clemence in *The Grandissimes*, Joy is like her in being a symbol of the slave masses; she is not, like Phyllis, an exotic exception to the generality. Joy accuses Ramsey in particular and the whites in general of not believing that "niggehs is got feelin's." Ramsey denies the charge, but Joy persists: "Some o' de bes' *believes* dey believes, dat's all. Oh I 'llow you, lots o' white folks is got . . . mo' feelin's dan some

niggehs; but lots o' niggehs is got *lots* mo' feelin's dan some
white folks. Mo' an' betteh!"

Although Cable's initial sympathy for the slave—prompted by
high-minded sentimentality and unconscious sensuality—centered
on the plight of quadroon and octoroon women, reason led him
to see that the principal sufferers were the Negro masses.
Blacks, not quadroons, serve as protagonists of the unimportant
antislavery stories, "The Angel of the Lord" and "The Clock in
the Sky," which he published in 1901. And an old black man,
Ovide Landry, not a glamorous woman of mixed blood, is the
spokesman for the Negro in the two novels that close Cable's
long career.

By the time his campaign for Negro rights ended in the
early 1890's, if not before, Cable shared the South's professed
abhorrence of interbreeding and intermarriage among Negroes
and whites, although his fiction continued to endorse other
mixed marriages. "The Angel of the Lord" specifically disap-
proves mixing the races as does *Gideon's Band,* written a dozen
years later. In the novel a quixotic Californian, struck by the
beauty of Phyllis and undisturbed by her stormy history, offers
to buy her, free her, and take her to the West as his wife.
With Cable's approval, he withdraws the offer in deference to
the general sense of outrage it produces. Cable's fiction
violates history in denying the colored victims any escape from
the stigma of their race except that provided by proof, real or
pretended, that they are really white. At the end of his career
he is so careful to avoid anything that smacks of a Negro-white
marriage that he makes a celibate of Fortune, a white girl
illegally held as a slave, when he tells her story in *The Flower
of the Chapdelaines.* Supposing herself to be colored, she is,
says one of the Creole characters, "too good and high-mind' to
be marrie' to any white man wha'z willin' to marry a nigger"; and,
like Phyllis and all the quadroons and octoroons in Cable's
canon, she can make no alliance with a man of the subject race
she has been taught to scorn. But late in the 1880's, when
Cable wrote of the real white slave, Salome Müller, in *Strange
True Stories of Louisiana,* he revealed that before she discovered
her identity and married a white man she was the mother of
several quadroon children.

II *The Flower of the Chapdelaines*

For *The Flower of the Chapdelaines,* published in 1918, Cable tied together revised versions of "A West Indian Slave Insurrection," "The Clock in the Sky," and "The Angel of the Lord" in a narrative framework that permitted him to relate these ante-bellum stories to one another and to depict Creole New Orleans of World War I. "The Clock in the Sky," which first appeared in *Scribner's Magazine,* September, 1901, is an effective but dated antislavery piece that smacks of Harriet Beecher Stowe. The narrator is a young Northern girl, the daughter of an abolitionist, who is visiting her beloved aunt and uncle in the South. The slave maid assigned to serve her is a pious girl who, despite her "amazing blackness," has "not one of the physical traits that so often make her race uncomely." As much as she loves her kindly master and mistress, her soul feels bondage "as her body would have felt a harrow." To escape being sold at auction, she and her parents and her brother Mingo run off in the night and follow the North Star to freedom.

The adventures of the fugitives on their way to the North are told in "The Angel of the Lord," a labored, melodramatic sequel unworthy of comparison with Cable's best fiction but not uncharacteristic of the narratives he produced during the years when he hoped to see his works presented on the stage. The story made its first appearance in 1901 in *A House Party,* a collection of twelve anonymous tales. The publishers offered a thousand-dollar prize to the reader who could identify the authors from a list of twenty-five American writers who had been invited to contribute to the volume. The measures Cable took to conceal his authorship add to the story's serious structural weaknesses, which he did not succeed in correcting in the version he included in *The Flower of the Chapdelaines.*

The young Southern lawyer who is the narrator of "The Angel of the Lord" comes upon the fugitive Negroes at a moment when he has disguised himself as a woman in order to play a joke on a friend. The girl of "amazing blackness" is also in disguise—as a boy—but her costume cannot conceal her piety or diminish a charm so great that it overcomes the narrator's professed abhorrence of Negroes. He changes clothes with the girl to confuse the pursuers, shoots the hounds that attack the party, and accompanies the slaves on their long journey to freedom. All reach the North except the worthless Mingo, who, like the Baron in "The Entomologist," is brought to grief by his appetite. "In broad noon, with an overseer and his gang plainly in sight in an adjoining cornfield, his self-command crumbled away under the seductions of a melon patch, and he howled away his freedom in the grip of a bear trap set for such slaves of appetite as he."

The hero of *The Flower of the Chapdelaines* is also a young lawyer, Geoffrey Chester, a Southerner but a stranger to New Orleans; Aline Chapdelaine, the heroine, is a Creole.[2] Aline and her maiden aunts hope to relieve their destitution by finding a publisher for old family manuscripts. Chester puts these in literary form, as Cable had done for Mrs. Miller's documents, and acts as agent. The manuscripts—the three stories included in the novel—are rejected. So is the absurd request of the aunts that they be allowed to ease Aline's burdens by entering an orphan asylum. The fortunes of the Chapdelaines are saved by the prosperous lawyer's marriage to Aline, his "unspeakable treasure."

Though Cable's approach to his material is partly that of the social critic, the narrative is little more than what Aline's mother would have called another "pretty pebble" from the Vieux Carré. The frame story features the usual autobiographical matter, and there are allusions to characters introduced in earlier books. Lacking a dramatic conflict and relying for its development on dialogue rather than on action, the novel is weak in structure; and this deficiency is not obscured, as it is in some of Cable's other books, by the pervasive charm of an intruding author. His scene is both the new New Orleans and the old. His Creoles use telephones and attend the movies; their sons are flying planes on the western front. As interested as they are in the fighting in Europe, they do not equate freedom for the slave and civil rights for the Negro citizen with the struggle for democracy abroad. They admire Aline's father and grandfather, who were active liberals "set, in conscience, against the conscience of their day," but they are conservatives themselves. Through Ovide Landry, a learned black bookseller, Cable challenges the notion that all Negro leaders during Reconstruction were ignorant and corrupt; his biography included in a recent book about whites, Ovide's honors are not all in the past. But because Cable was writing for a *"publique . . .* not any longer pretty easy to fascinate" on the subject of Negro rights, he beats the dead horse, slavery, but hardly shakes an admonishing finger at the contemporary South.

III *Lovers of Louisiana*

Even so, *The Flower of the Chapdelaines,* which links the problems and attitudes of the present with the heritage of the past, is Cable's second step on the road back to social criticism. The first was *Gideon's Band,* in which he resumed his condemnation of slavery and caste and decried the real ante-bellum Southern culture that apologists had idealized in the plantation tradition. These two books, mild in their social criticism and looking toward the past, echo his earliest writing. But his final novel, published in September of 1918, was intended as a manifesto for the future. Cable meant *Lovers of Louisiana* to be a political work, just as he had meant *The Grandissimes* to be. The veteran novelist, as Randolph Bourne remarked in his review in the *Dial,* gave it the flavor of romance but poured into it an astonishing intellectuality.

Spokesmen for the author are a visiting Scot named Murray and the men of a distinguished Southern family of New Orleans' Nouveau Quartier, the Castletons. Father, son, and grandfather, the Castletons are a trinity; each man is an idealization of Cable himself but each enjoys a status Cable had never quite attained. Philip Castleton's deceased father is the martyr Cable would have been had he remained in New Orleans and battled the evils he saw there instead of exiling himself in the North and forsaking reform and social criticism for innocuous civic benevolence and routine romance. Pilloried for his assaults on lynching and the Ku Klux Klan, Philip's father was heartbroken, as Cable had been in the days of the Open Letter Club, to find "Northerners . . . uninterested and compliant and Southerners . . . eager to tell what the South must never, never do or suffer to be done."

Philip Castleton is the man Cable was just before he moved away from New Orleans and the man Cable would have wanted

which studied the city's prisons and asylums in 1881. Only
author's habit of dramatizing the plight of the subject
by representing its exploitation in sexual relationships—the
ed woman at the mercy of the white male—can account
éphire's attempted abduction of a quadroon girl in a city
e prostitution had flourished openly for forty years.

Lovers of Louisiana has less charm than Old Creole Days,
nodern American city, more prosaic than the old Latin one,
share the blame with the author. If the novel's characters
stereotyped, credit must be given to Cable's achievement
aking his earlier Creoles and quadroons such vital, memor-
figures as to become established prototypes. If his plot
on a dream vision, strained coincidences, and other
ard contrivances of romance, Cable is no more to be held
ntable than his public and his colleagues.

vers of Louisiana was written when serious literature was
e doldrums in the United States. The era of quality
zines purveying fine writing to a refined audience was
The newer national magazines turned away from muckrak-
nd reform by the end of the first decade of the twentieth
ry. Mark Twain was dead. Henry James and William
Howells, the former forgotten and the latter, by his own
ssion, "a comparatively dead cult," had published their
iction. Theodore Dreiser, Ellen Glasgow, Willa Cather,
Edith Wharton were making significant contributions to
ican literature; but the public preferred the work of Mary
ton, John Fox, Jr., Gene Stratton Porter, Harold Bell
ht, and Kate Douglas Wiggin.

e cause of Negro rights, for which Cable had once labored
ally, could make little headway against the popularity of
Birth of a Nation (1915), the movie dramatization of
as Dixon's race-baiting novel, The Clansman.[4] Despite
pirit of the times, Cable made his final book a testimonial
abiding devotion to public morality, civic benevolence,
olitical idealism. Lovers of Louisiana goes far toward mak-
ments for the vapid romances and trivial miscellany Cable
in his Richard Thorndyke Smith period. With this last
Cable gave the final touches to his portrait of a milieu
s really his alone in American literary history.

his son to be had one grown to maturity. Like Cable, Philip
believes that "a true lover of his city . . . must do his finest
to help fit her for a high place in the world—oh, better—for a
high place in the world's service!" When he speaks out on the
race problem, Philip is treated as Cable had been: snubbed on
the street, challenged to a duel, threatened with a cowhiding.
Aware of the disadvantages of self-educated intelligence, Cable
gives Philip formal qualifications for his intellectuality—a Ph.D.
degree in history from Princeton—and makes him a member of
the Tulane faculty.

Philip's grandfather, whose youthful features show "repose,
benevolence, and intrepidity," is such a man as Cable must
have wished his own father had been. Judge Castleton's love
affair with the heroine's grand'mère helps make a Gordian knot
in the silken "thread of absurd punctilio" that keeps Philip and
Rosalie Durel apart. It seems significant also as an intimation
of an amorous spirit so unflagging as to lead Cable to marry
for the third time at the age of seventy-nine.

The Durels, whose social eminence in New Orleans is equal
to that of the Castletons, live in the Vieux Carré. Kept apart
at home by "different languages, religions, literatures, moral
standards, [and] social codes," the two families meet on vacation
in Atlantic City; here Philip immediately falls in love with the
daughter of the Creole banker. M. Durel considers any
Américain—particularly Philip—an unwelcome suitor for his
daughter's hand. The Creole has not forgotten that, when years
ago he paid court to Philip's mother, her family regarded him
as unacceptable because of his religion. Philip's rival is a wanton
cashier, Zéphire, whose embezzlement nearly ruins Durel's bank.
The proud Durels are further humiliated by the discovery that
the Castletons, at great sacrifice, have loaned them the money
to make good the loss. Philip cannot press his suit until money
from the gods permits the Creole banker to repay the loan.
Cleared of all obstacles except Philip's unorthodox principles,
which the Durels have become enlightened enough to tolerate,
the road to marriage stretches out before the young lovers.

Philip's unpopularity in his native city stems from his belief
that he can be "a good Southerner" only by being "an American
citizen on the American plan." Though his articles are evidently
mild in their censure of "poor Dixie's well-meant mistakes,"

he is roughly handled by the press. Loyal New Orleanians, especially Creoles, cannot but be offended by a man who calls the Mardi Gras a "tawdry lunacy" difficult to excuse, an "organized old puerility—which is neither reality nor good dreamstuff, celebrates no achievement, initiates no enterprise, presents no contest of strength or skill, and offers no illustration worth saving overnight of any art, literature, or other refinement."[3] Philip's greatest infraction of the Southern code is his request that the members of the literary society at the Negro college forget, as he addresses them, that he is white. This seeming disloyalty to his race is the fictional equivalent of Cable's act of eating with Negroes in Nashville in 1889, the indiscretion that killed his Open Letter Club.

In sharp contrast to the forthright stand on Negro rights Cable had taken in his speech to the literary society at Vanderbilt in 1887, Philip advises his black and "half-and-half" listeners to make themselves "privately so estimable and publicly so valuable that the few rights yet denied you will come by natural gravitation if not to you to your children's children." This gradualism is received with faint applause by people whose ancestors had made their home in America for three hundred years and who, fifty years after attaining the legal rights of citizenship, found themselves, as Philip acknowledged, "half-way down again to . . . slavery."

On controversies less likely than the race question to estrange Philip from the reader's sympathies or to endanger his appeal as hero, Cable lets him take a more positive stand. Speaking always as though he were in the pulpit or on the rostrum at a political convention, Philip announces himself in favor of votes for women because there should be "the same political freedom between man and woman as between man and man." With war raging in Europe, he looks to a supra-national body to establish and maintain world peace. He does not mention lynching, but he does say that "all overriding of law by violence is a criminal and infamous attack on public safety, honor, and liberty." Philip talks of writing—as his father had hoped to do— a small, earnest book detailing what the South must accomplish "socially, politically, in order to fill her place in the world's and America's progress"; but in the novel he defines his principles no more than to say they are derived from "the Constitution,

Lover of Louisiana

the Declaration, and the Moral Law." Th[...] seems no more radical than that of the minist[...] sin, in Louisiana it is enough to make Philip[...]

Some of the other characters speak Cable'[...] than does his native white Southern protag[...] a new accent, Scottish, to the many linguisti[...] Cable had insisted over the years that the[...] an exclusively Southern or American phenom[...] and solved. Ovide Landry, whose import[...] outweighs his role in *The Flower of the* [...] Murray in reciting Cable's basic premise:[...] treated in accordance with their individual[...] are the Holdens, the family of the presiden[...] college for Negroes, Northerners who call [...] and treat colored people as their social equal[...] of the Castletons as well as the Durels. T[...] Murray, Ovide, the Holdens—compose a cho[...] political philosophy. The refrain is the [...] citizen to make the New Testament his pol[...] his city—his section, his country—as he doe[...] show that love by devoting his energies to [...] Cable's last effort as a storyteller is his final[...] like himself, profess to love Louisiana.

Louisiana, which he said forty years earl[...] *simes* had "grown up out of joint," meant for [...] a city placed at a disadvantage, Frowen[...] "distant from enlightened centres." Though[...] of *Lovers of Louisiana* occurs in Atlantic [...] Bermuda, Cable's scene is still the Crescent [...] of 1915, with its telephones and movies and[...] the picturesque city of 1803; but it is still,[...] remarks, "the mother city of an antiquated [...] the nation and the world."

A novelist in his seventies can hardly b[...] forward to new materials or new methods, [...] that Cable's final novel is more a summary[...] in the past than a vigorous application of [...] explicit problems of contemporary New O[...] tion of *clairvoyantes* by the grand jury, he[...] pale reflection of Cable's experience as se[...]

IV *Last Years*

Two of Cable's concerns in his declining years were the League of Nations and world peace. In Northampton he spoke to the Social and Literary Club on "International Federation" in 1915 and on "Permanent Peace" at a meeting in November, 1918, the last he attended before his resignation the following year. He was rarely in Northampton when the club met because he and his wife now spent the winters in a milder climate. It was in Bermuda that a friend of Charles W. Chesnutt's family accidentally came upon Cable in January, 1922. She wrote Helen M. Chesnutt, a Smith College graduate who had taught at the Home Culture clubhouse and had known Cable in Northampton, that the little man "darted, rather than walked onto the porch. One eye looked as if it were glass. He wore a gray smoking jacket or house coat, bound with black, shabby, decidedly worn braid." He offered to serve as guide, but "All at once in the midst of conversation he began to demonstrate the German goose step, insisting that I try it, too. So we went goose-stepping along." A few minutes later Cable darted away, "vanishing in just no time."[5]

He resigned from the Williston board of trustees because of failing health in November. After Mrs. Cable died in the following June, Cable went to Northampton to live with his youngest daughter and her family. In December, 1923, he married Mrs. Hanna Cowing, whom he described as a friend of the family for thirty-five years. Before her marriage to Cable, Mrs. Cowing sometimes entertained favored boarders at her home at 32 Paradise Road, just a few steps away from "Tarryawhile," with long fireside tales about the noted author. She and Cable spent that winter in St. Petersburg, Florida, and it was there, on January 31, 1925, that he died. He was in his eighty-first year. Cable's body was sent to Northampton, where he was buried beside his first wife. William Allan Neilson, president of Smith College, read a funeral tribute that gave equal attention to Cable's distinction as an author and to his contributions to the welfare of the community that was his adopted home and final resting place.

As Cable had hoped, both sprawling New Orleans and tidy

Northampton were indebted to him, though neither city has chosen to pay its respects in a significant and tangible way. New Orleans, always the home of his imagination, remained the subject of most of his fiction long after he had left it. There he is remembered as an artist celebrated in his day as the greatest Southern writer since Poe and as one who made the scenes of his birthplace familiar to readers across the country; but New Orleanians do not hold him in affection because they remember also what Randolph Bourne called his "fatally critical sense of the poisons that continued to beset the South's convalescence."[6] His efforts to drive the South to abandon its undemocratic practices, modernize its institutions, and rid itself of corruption made him an alien.

Northampton he found to be a thoroughly compatible society that respected his achievements as a man of letters and approved his projects for civic betterment. But the Northern city never fired his spirit—it seemed to him typical rather than unique, prosaic rather than provocatively quaint—and its social problems left him emotionally unaffected. Many people in Northampton who use the facilities of The People's Institute, now a Red Feather agency, have never heard of Cable, since no building is named for him. Visitors may easily fail to notice the picture of the founder, donated by the third Mrs. Cable, which hangs in the lobby of "Carnegie House." "Tarryawhile," now simply 23 Dryads' Green, is in private hands, as is the study, built around 1904, now 21 Dryads' Green. The remains of Cable's garden may still be seen, and some of the memorial trees planted on his grounds are standing, unmarked. Yet his determined service to the city is appropriately commemorated in the continuing operations of The People's Institute at "Carnegie House" and "James House," however rarely these activities may be associated with his name.

In New Orleans, now that his voice is no longer raised in outcry against its history and sacred institutions, Cable is almost —though not quite—forgiven. Certainly there is lingering resentment on the part of Creoles understandably sensitive about his presentation of the foibles and occasional moral lapses of some of their ancestors. Just as Baedeker's 1904 *Handbook to the United States* completed its guide to the city with quotations from Cable's books and admonitions to the tourist to read his stories, modern guide books point out to Mardi Gras visitors the buildings featured in Cable's Creole tales. But it is the quaintness of the Vieux Carré rather than the artistic achievement of the man who wrote about it that is the source of civic pride, and the launching of a Liberty Ship named in his honor is hardly an appropriate or permanent tribute. New Orleanians prefer to read the more comforting stories of Grace King or Lyle Saxon, though they identify for the tourist the scenes George W. Cable immortalized.

V *Appraisals of Cable*

The minor position presently assigned to Cable in American literary history by many scholars does not accord with his importance during the years that followed his removal from the South. In 1884 a *Critic* list of "Forty Immortals" ranked G. W. Cable and Henry James behind William Dean Howells, who was fifth, but ahead of Mark Twain, who was fourteenth. A cartoon in *Life*, May 27, 1897, depicting the ten most popular authors of the day, exaggerated Cable's diminutive stature and placed in his hand a manuscript marked "Georgie Cable's Creole Songs for Tenor." In 1899 Howells was first, Twain second, and Cable tenth on a list of the greatest living American writers selected by readers of the U.S. edition of *Literature. The Cavalier* sold a hundred thousand copies between October 5 and Christmas, 1901, more than twenty years after critics had acclaimed Cable a major American author, worthy to stand beside Poe and Hawthorne and the European masters of fiction. Presumably, his name was still familiar to *Life* readers in 1917, when "A Song for France" appeared in the issue for May 24. In 1920, two years after the appearance of the books that closed his long career, *Old Creole Days,* first published in 1879, sold more than five hundred copies.

Longfellow's *Ultima Thule* appeared in the year that Cable's first novel was issued in book form; T. S. Eliot's *Prufrock and Other Observations* was in print before Cable's last two books went on sale. He was celebrated as the first Southern novelist to make a permanent contribution to the nation's literature by the time Colonel William Falkner's *The White Rose of Memphis* became a best seller in 1881; within a month after Cable died in 1925, leaving among his papers the manuscript of an unfinished novel about New Orleans Creoles after World War I, the Colonel's grandson, William Faulkner, was contributing New Orleans sketches to the *Times-Picayune* and the *Double Dealer*, which was publishing in its pages the work of Ernest Hemingway, Sherwood Anderson, Hart Crane, John Crowe Ransom, Ezra Pound, and other writers soon to be famous.

The literary reputation of an author, particularly of one who is productive for nearly half a century, will fluctuate during his lifetime and, of course, will be affected by further changes in taste after his death. But the decline of Cable's literary status may be traced in part to non-literary considerations. One of these was continuing hostility toward works—Cable's best—that so confused public opinion about Creole purity of blood that a scholar like Fred Lewis Pattee could make the faux pas, in *A History of American Literature Since 1870*, of speaking of "Creoles of the quadroon type" and grouping Aurora Nancanou with Madame Delphine. Another was Cable's aggressive agitation for Negro rights in articles that were lamented as dissipations of his artistic energies or attacked as misguided polemics. Sophisticated Southern readers today take more pride in the saga of Yoknapatawpha County—hardly a flattering creation— than in Margaret Mitchell's *Gone With the Wind*, with all its magnolias and crinoline and sectional heroism. Hamilton Basso, Tennessee Williams, and Robert Penn Warren acknowledge in their work many of the unsavory realities of Southern life. But these authors, and others like them, have not made the mistake of campaigning in non-fiction against the regional practices established by their forebears and regarded as sacrosanct by their contemporaries. Cable's essays, however, condemned Southern mistreatment of Negroes and poor whites; Southern scorn of the immigrant; and Southern ambitions to create a modern, industrial society while refusing even to consider enlightened principles of human relations. The South barred its platforms to the renegade. It closed its eyes and ears to Cable's message.

The North did much the same. Cable's earliest fiction was approved by readers appreciative of the evidences that the author was properly reconstructed—by readers who remembered John W. De Forest's *Miss Ravenel's Conversion from Secession to Loyalty* (1867) and *Kate Beaumont* (1872). But soon Southern writers, abetted by Northern editors, established in the national mind an idyllic image of the ante-bellum period as a time when happy slaves frolicked in the shadow of a stately portico. Thomas Nelson Page's "Marse Chan" appeared in *Century Magazine* in April, 1884; *In Ole Virginia* was published in 1887. The plantation tradition established by Page and his followers was appealing to the North, which was anxious to be done with the controversy that had wracked the country. The issue Cable raised, the civil status of the ex-slave, was one the nation was now willing to leave to the South. Even those readers who respected Cable's dedication to the lost cause of the freedman called on him for picturesque stories of olden times. The public failed to recognize and neglected to encourage the strength of his social vision and his talent for realistic portrayal of regional experience.

Yet it is just these qualities, which he displayed magnificently in some books but obscured or held in abeyance in others, that distinguish Cable's finest work and constitute his contribution to American literature. Beneath a surface delicacy and quaintness that misled careless readers into thinking he was interested primarily in sentiment and romance, Cable gave an incisive picture of the social and political situations with which he was deeply concerned. Although his scene often appeared to be the New Orleans of a bygone time, "he supposed himself," as Edmund Wilson has said, "to be dealing with the realities of contemporary life—and this was true."[7] No appraisal of his work is just if it fails to acknowledge the importance of his achievement and to commend him for it.

Notes and References

Chapter One

1. "Creole" is used in this book, in accordance with Cable's practice, to designate white persons descended from and preserving the culture of the French or Spanish settlers of New Orleans and the surrounding delta. Because other usages of the term were—and are—current, it remains a source of confusion to this day. In "The Ordeal of George Washington Cable," *New Yorker*, XXXIII (November 9, 1957), 174, Edmund Wilson says that "a Creole is a white colonial of French or Spanish blood" and adds that Cable's "non-Southern audience" was "misled" in thinking the word meant "a Frenchman with an admixture of Negro blood." On the other hand, Shirley Ann Grau indicates in her foreword to Cable's *Old Creole Days* (New York, 1961), p. viii, that the word was and is commonly used in New Orleans to designate "a person of French and Spanish ancestry, who may or may not have colored blood."

2. Edward Larocque Tinker, "Cable and the Creoles," in George W. Cable, *Old Creole Days* (New York, 1943), p. vii.

3. By 1860, when Cable was in his teens, "there were 9,877 free Negroes and 6,131 slaves in the two districts of the city which were largely composed of Latin Creoles and immigrant Catholics. The free Negroes in this area, the 'Creoles de couleur,' were predominantly Catholic and the same is true, judging from records in the St. Louis Cathedral archives, of the slaves." Robert C. Reinders, "The Churches and the Negro in New Orleans, 1850-1860," *Phylon*, XXII (Third Quarter, 1961), 242n.

4. The poems are reprinted in *Creole Voices: Poems in French by Free Men of Color, First Published in 1845*, ed. by Edward Maceo Coleman (Washington, 1945). That the poets have little or nothing to say about slavery, their own caste, New Orleans, or America is easily explained. Law and custom prohibited attacks on slavery; the authors thought of themselves as French; and some of them were slaveholders.

5. The Cable family freed its slaves in Pennsylvania. Evidently neither this act nor the Northern ancestry of Rebecca Boardman Cable led G. W. Cable's parents to conclude that slavery was wrong. The family held slaves during his childhood in New Orleans.

6. The demand for national self-consciousness in literature continued for many years. For a late but representative expression of

this point of view, see Hamilton W. Mabie, "American Literature and American Nationality," *Forum*, XXVI (January, 1899), 636-38.

7. The letter appears in Lucy Leffingwell Cable's "The Story of the Author's Life," in *The Cable Story Book*, ed. by Mary E. Burt and Lucy Leffingwell Cable (New York, 1899), p. 167.

8. The extant letters of Cable and Boyesen, from which I quote in this study, are printed, with some omissions, in Arlin Turner, "A Novelist Discovers a Novelist: The Correspondence of H. H. Boyesen and George W. Cable," *Western Humanities Review*, V (Autumn, 1951), 343-72. See also Kjell Ekström, "Cable's *Grandissimes* and the Creoles," *Studia Neophilologica*, XXI (Autumn, 1949), 190-94.

Chapter Two

1. Cable refrains from establishing the girl's identity unequivocally, just as he does in the case of 'Tite Poulette. Is 'Sieur George's denial of blood relationship to his ward a part of the "senseless act" he attempts to commit? When Cable has him break his "good resolution" by making the proposal of marriage he has been contemplating "for months," the incipient sensuality of the story threatens, at the moment of climax, to become overt and dominant.

2. The question of the accuracy and generosity of Cable's portrait of the Creole is treated at length in Kjell Ekström, *George Washington Cable: A Study of His Early Life and Work* (Cambridge, Mass., 1950), pp. 111-84. See also Griffith T. Pugh, "George W. Cable's Theory and Use of Folk Speech," *Southern Folklore Quarterly*, XXIV (December, 1960), 287-93.

3. Here, in Cable's earliest Creole story, is the progenitor of the Anglo-Saxon protagonists of later works, especially Dutch Kristian Koppig of "'Tite Poulette" and German Joseph Frowenfeld of *The Grandissimes*.

4. The house that served as prototype for the De Charleu mansion was the Zeringue place on the other side of the Mississippi. It was still standing when Lafcadio Hearn wrote "The Scenes of Cable's Romances," published in *Century Magazine* in November, 1883, almost ten years after the first appearance of Cable's story.

5. Edward Stone, "Usher, Poquelin, and Miss Emily: The Progress of Southern Gothic," *Georgia Review*, XIV (Winter, 1960), 438.

6. Only in *Strange True Stories of Louisiana* does Cable acknowledge that there were instances of miscegenation in which the male, rather than the female, was colored. No quadroon or octoroon woman in his canon marries a man of her own or a darker caste.

Yet visiting Edward King did not think it astonishing to see in Cable's New Orleans "a smart-looking young negro man with a quadroon wife." "Old and New Louisiana," *Scribner's Monthly,* VII (December, 1873), 141.

7. Mary Cable Dennis, *The Tail of the Comet* (New York, 1937), p. 61.

Chapter Three

1. *The Great Tradition* (New York, 1933), p. 52.

2. Nursing is a plot device in many of Cable's narratives. "His plots are little more than sentimental situations, some of which he used over and over again in slightly different forms." W. Adolphe Roberts, *Lake Pontchartrain* (New York, 1946), p. 281.

3. "Citizen of the Union," *New Republic,* LVII (February 13, 1929), 352.

4. The main Grandissime line has always been "lily-white," Cable says, "—as to marriage, that is; as to less responsible entanglements, why, of course—"

5. In *Manon Lescaut* (1731), the Abbé Prévost's famous novel about a chevalier and a courtesan, the lovers take refuge in America but find New Orleans disappointing. They watch as the governor inspects the girls who have arrived with them from France. The prettiest he gives as wives to leading young men of the town; lesser men cast lots for the others.

6. Newton Arvin, "Introduction," in George W. Cable, *The Grandissimes* (New York, 1957), p. x.

7. For example, free men of color, unlike slaves, could obtain patents for inventions. Several did so, among them "a colored Creole of Louisiana" who patented a number of devices important to the sugar industry. Henry E. Baker, "The Negro in the Field of Invention," *Journal of Negro History,* II (January, 1917), 25.

8. Boston *Evening Transcript,* June 15, 1882. Although Cable once said he retained few impressions from his boyhood reading of *Uncle Tom's Cabin,* he may have been especially affected by Mrs. Stowe's picture of Cassy, a New Orleans quadroon. In the woman's appearance and character there is much that suggests Cable's quadroons, particularly Palmyre.

9. "A Note on Mr. Cable's 'The Grandissimes,'" *Bookman,* VII (July, 1898), 403.

Chapter Four

1. Père Jerome seems a perfect answer to M. B. Morse, who compared Cable's work with that of Dickens, Thackeray, Hugo, and Scott but lamented that he did not depict Catholics more favorably.

"The Louisiana of Creole Days," *Catholic World*, XXXII (January, 1881), 463-72.

2. Letter to his mother, July 19, 1875, in Lucy Leffingwell Cable Biklé, *George W. Cable: His Life and Letters* (New York, 1928), p. 53.

3. Letter to his wife, June 4, 1881, *ibid.*, p. 66.

4. Letter to his wife, June 24, 1881, *ibid.*, p. 70.

5. "George W. Cable," *Century Magazine*, XXIII (February, 1882), 604-5.

6. Julia Collier Harris, *The Life and Letters of Joel Chandler Harris* (Boston, 1918), pp. 570-71.

7. Four years later, on August 7, 1887, Cable wrote Howells: "I am troubled to see a paragraph floating around in the newspapers stating that in a late lecture I had criticized your work and particularly had picked some flaw about the mention by you of the typewriter." This time Cable was free to make an outright denial of the reputed indiscretion, because, as he pointed out, his speech was "not reported in shorthand." Kjell Ekström, "The Cable-Howells Correspondence," *Studia Neophilologica*, XXII (Spring, 1950), 56-57.

8. Kenneth R. Andrews, *Nook Farm: Mark Twain's Hartford Circle* (Cambridge, Mass., 1950), p. 99.

9. Twain to Howells, November 4, 1882, in *Mark Twain-Howells Letters*, ed. by Henry Nash Smith and William M. Gibson (Cambridge, Mass., 1960), I, 419.

10. See his letter to Mark Twain, March 10, 1883, in my *George W. Cable: The Northampton Years* (New York, 1959), pp. 12-13. Cable did not hesitate to describe his platform appearances as triumphs. See his letter to Twain, June 29, 1882, in Guy A. Cardwell, *Twins of Genius* (East Lansing, Mich., 1953), p. 83, and his letter to Daniel C. Gilman, November 22, 1883, in Biklé, *op. cit.*, pp. 108-9.

11. The address is printed in Arlin Turner, "George W. Cable's Revolt Against Literary Sectionalism," *Tulane Studies in English*, V (1955), 8-24.

Chapter Five

1. For Cable's comments on the origin and pronunciation of the name, see the newspaper interview reprinted in part in Fred W. Lorch, "Cable and His Reading Tour with Mark Twain in 1884-1885," *American Literature*, XXIII (January, 1952), 481. Cable remarked that the name was common in Tennessee, but he did not mention that the first governor of the state was named John Sevier.

2. Twain complained, in the notebook he kept on the tour, that there was too much of Cable on the program. A dozen years later he

recorded in another notebook the charge that Cable "stole" platform time on their tour. Paul Fatout, "The Twain-Cable Readings in Indiana," *Indiana Magazine of History*, LIII (March, 1957), 23.

3. Arlin Turner, *George W. Cable: A Biography* (Durham, N. C., 1956), p. 152.

4. "Mark Twain," *Century Magazine*, XXIV (September, 1882), 780.

5. The popular series brought sensational increases in the magazine's circulation. *Battles and Leaders of the Civil War*, 4 vols., ed. by Robert Underwood Johnson and Clarence Clough Buel (New York, 1887), served Stephen Crane as one of the sources for *The Red Badge of Courage*.

6. Hal Holbrook, *Mark Twain Tonight!* (New York, 1959), p. 93. In his unsigned review of Twain's novel, Brander Matthews praised Jim as worthy to rank with Cable's Bras-Coupé. London *Saturday Review*, LIX, (January 31, 1885), 154.

7. Letter, September 17, 1884, in *Mark Twain-Howells Letters*, ed. by Henry Nash Smith and William M. Gibson (Cambridge, Mass., 1960), II, 509-10.

8. William S. Scarborough, head of the Classical Department at Wilberforce University in Ohio at the time *Huckleberry Finn* was written, might possibly have served as Twain's inspiration for the Negro professor.

9. Mary Cable Dennis, *The Tail of the Comet* (New York, 1937), p. 74. There is very little swearing in Cable's earliest books. It increases in *John March, Southerner* and in the Civil War romances.

10. Twain to his wife, February 5, 1885, quoted in part in Guy A. Cardwell, *Twins of Genius* (East Lansing, Mich., 1953), p. 55.

11. James M. Cox, "Walt Whitman, Mark Twain, and the Civil War," *Sewanee Review*, LXIX (April-June, 1961), 203.

Chapter Six

1. Cable to his wife, January 7, 1885, in Arlin Turner, *Mark Twain and George W. Cable* (East Lansing, Mich., 1960), p. 85. Cable not only assumed the mantle of the abolitionists; it was conferred on him. William Still, a Philadelphia Negro who had been an important abolitionist, wrote on November 7, 1888, inviting Cable to address a meeting of the Pennsylvania Society for Promoting the Abolition of Slavery to be held in January to celebrate the twenty-fifth anniversary of emancipation. Other speakers were to be Frederick Douglass, Booker T. Washington, and General Samuel C. Armstrong,

founder of Hampton Institute. The letter is in the Cable Collection at Tulane University.

2. An editor of the Atlanta *Constitution,* Grady attained a reputation as orator and spokesman for the New South. In an article on Cable, James B. Whiple remarks that in a speech in which Grady praised the Negro as "contented . . . the companion of the hunt and frolic, the furrow and the home," he might as well have been talking about his dog. "Southern Rebel," *Phylon,* XX (Fourth Quarter, 1959), 352 and note.

3. Turner, *op. cit.,* p. 94.

4. *Daily Hampshire Gazette,* December 22, 1936.

5. *Quarter Centennial Hampshire County Journal,* October, 1887, p. 48.

6. Cable's only mistake was in having a row of willow saplings planted as a screen between the gymnasium and the residences in its rear. The saplings attracted a swarm of caterpillars that spread to neighboring gardens. Public protests forced the removal of the screen. Many of the other plantings Cable directed survived until the institution moved to a new campus in 1951.

7. See Arlin Turner, *George W. Cable: A Biography* (Durham, N. C., 1956), p. 230, for a passage on the brutal treatment of slaves that Cable's editors expunged. These two essays are reprinted in *Creoles and Cajuns: Stories of Old Louisiana by George W. Cable,* ed. by Arlin Turner (Garden City, N. Y., 1959).

Chapter Seven

1. Cable's essay, "The Negro Question in the United States," was issued as a pamphlet, *The Negro Question,* by the American Missionary Association. Several of his later articles on the race problem were published as pamphlets, by the American Missionary Association and other organizations, for distribution in the South.

2. Most of Adelene Moffat's letters to Cable are in the Cable Collection at Tulane University. His letters to her are in the Cable Collection at Columbia University.

3. Park Street is now called Trumbull Road.

4. Cable made a short contribution to the Open Letter Club symposium, "Shall the Negro Be Educated or Suppressed?" which appeared in the *Independent,* February 21, 1889. The club distributed the symposium, somewhat enlarged, as a pamphlet. The original essays in the *Independent* and Seth Low's contribution to the pamphlet are reprinted in the 1895 edition of Atticus G. Haygood's *Our Brother in Black: His Freedom and His Future* (Nashville), pp. 269-98.

5. Cable discusses his method of constructing characters from models in "After-Thoughts of a Story-Teller," *North American Review*, CLVIII (January, 1894), 16-23.

6. Cable's letter to the editor of the *Literary World*, May 31, 1875, is in the Berg Collection of the New York Public Library. See my *George W. Cable: The Northampton Years* (New York, 1959), pp. 8-9.

7. There was substantial racial integration in New Orleans schools for more than six years during Reconstruction. See Louis R. Harlan, "Desegregation in New Orleans Public Schools during Reconstruction," *American Historical Review*, LXVII (April, 1962), 663-75.

8. Only one of the letters was published in the newspaper, September 26, 1875. Both are printed in *The Negro Question*, ed. by Arlin Turner (Garden City, N. Y., 1958), pp. 27-33.

Chapter Eight

1. The volume is composed of "The Negro Question" (New York *Tribune*, March 4, 1888, and elsewhere); "National Aid to Southern Schools" (published as "A National Debt" in the Minneapolis *Northwestern Congregationalist*, September, 1889); "What Shall the Negro Do?" (*Forum*, August, 1888); "A Simpler Southern Question" (*Forum*, December, 1888); "What Makes the Color Line?" (Chicago *America*, June 13, 1889); and "The Southern Struggle for Pure Government" (abridged as "Equal Rights in the South," New York *Tribune*, February 23, 1890, and elsewhere, and published as a pamphlet by the Massachusetts Club, 1890).

2. One version of "My Politics," with some deletions, may be found in *The Negro Question*, ed. by Arlin Turner (Garden City, N. Y., 1958), pp. 2-25.

3. Mary Cable Dennis, *The Tail of the Comet* (New York, 1937), p. 160.

4. Cable was evidently the author of a document, signed by about two hundred Northampton citizens, praising Lyman's benevolence and thanking him for the gift. Cable's name heads the list of signers, and he served as authority for writing in fourteen other names. The document is in the archives of the Northampton Historical Society.

5. Springfield (Mass.) *Republican*, December 8, 1894.

6. Louis D. Rubin, Jr., "The Road to Yoknapatawpha," *Virginia Quarterly Review*, XXXV (Winter, 1959), 120.

7. This comment from Cable's diary is quoted in Arlin Turner, *George W. Cable: A Biography* (Durham, N. C., 1956), p. 279.

8. "From an Older Time," *Dial*, LXV (November 2, 1918), 364.

9. *Ibid.*

10. Cable to Twain, October 25, 1884, in Guy A. Cardwell, *Twins of Genius* (East Lansing, Mich., 1953), p. 105.

11. On the Reconstruction fiction of Page, Thomas Dixon, and other Southern writers, see Theodore L. Gross, "The Negro in the Literature of Reconstruction," *Phylon*, XXII (First Quarter, 1961), 5-14. Cable is quoted as praising Dixon's *The Leopard's Spots* (1902) in Kelly Miller, *Race Adjustment* (New York, 1908), p. 28.

12. The name may have been suggested to Cable by "Wildwood," a Northampton estate not far from his home. See Clarence Hawkes, "The Streets of Northampton," in *Northampton: The Meadow City* (Northampton, Mass., 1894), p. 90. Cable's signed article in this volume, "Paradise Woods," pp. 91-95, has not been included in bibliographies of his works.

13. Another contributor to Cable's plot may well have been Mark Twain, whose father left a hundred thousand acres of Tennessee land when he died. A scheme to make the land profitable by bringing in European immigrants who knew grape-growing and wine-making was abandoned because of objections from Orion Clemens, then interested in the temperance movement. Twain had made literary use of his inheritance in *The Gilded Age* (1873), with which Cable was familiar, and probably he mentioned it to Cable on their reading tour. See *The Autobiography of Mark Twain*, ed. by Charles Neider (New York, 1959), pp. 218-19.

14. *The Negro Question* (New York, 1890), pp. 141-43.

15. Arlin Turner, "George W. Cable, Novelist and Reformer," *South Atlantic Quarterly*, XLVIII (October, 1949), 544.

Chapter Nine

1. Clarence B. Roote noted in his diary on June 14, 1896, that, after soliciting his opinion of a recent manuscript by Anna H. Branch, then a Smith junior, Cable remarked that the poem gave promise the writer would become "as great a poet as America had yet produced." Roote's extant journals are the property of the George Holmes Bixby Memorial Library, Francestown, N. H.

2. Madeleine Wallin was a student at Smith from 1888 to 1890. After earning degrees from Minnesota and Chicago, she returned to Northampton as an assistant in history at Smith College from 1894 to 1896. In 1897 she married George Cushing Sikes of Chicago. Her comments about Cable in her letter to Adelene Moffat, April 9, 1907, are illuminating. The letter is in the Cable Collection at

Columbia University. Her extant letters to Cable are in the Cable Collection at Tulane University.

3. Clarence B. Roote's diary, June 29, 1896.

4. The true story of another Gulf island, a populated resort which was swept away by a tidal wave, Cable told at a dinner in New Orleans at which his erstwhile friend Lafcadio Hearn was present. Hearn later used Cable's description as one source for his poetic novel *Chita: A Memory of Last Island* (1889).

5. The essays featuring Richard Thorndyke Smith are: "The Speculations of a Story-Teller" (*Atlantic Monthly*, July, 1896); "Extracts from a Story-Teller's Dictionary" (*Chap-Book*, September 15, 1896); "To See Our Life as Romance Sees It" (*Symposium*, November, 1896); and "Art and Morals in Books" (*Independent*, December 16, 1897).

Chapter Ten

1. Certainly Smith deeply admires Ferry, but it seems extreme to say, as Edmund Wilson does, that the relations of these two "fall little short of the homosexual." "The Ordeal of George Washington Cable," *New Yorker*, XXXIII (November 9, 1957), 211.

2. A dozen years later the favor was returned. When the D. A. Sullivan School burned in February, 1914, the high school classes were housed for about thirteen months in the main building of the Home Culture Clubs, then renamed The People's Institute.

3. President Seelye of Smith College, probably encouraged by Cable's success, also appealed to Carnegie. Early in 1905 Seelye asked help in financing a new biological laboratory. At first Carnegie denied the request; but, after visiting Smith in connection with the dedication of "Carnegie House," he gave the college $125,000. Harriet Seelye Rhees, *Laurenus Clark Seelye* (Boston, 1929), pp. 227-28.

4. Personal letter to me from Harry B. Taplin, October 5, 1960.

5. Northampton *Herald*, April 13, 1905.

6. Hemenway described the organization and rules for the garden competition in his small book, *How to Make Home and City Beautiful* (Northampton, Mass., 1911), pp. 97-101. See Cable's "The Cottage Gardens of Northampton," *Youth's Companion*, LXXXV (April 13, 1911), 190-91 (incorporated in *The Amateur Garden*).

7. Mary K. Brewster's journals, January 1, 1907. In my possession. A direct descendant of Pilgrim William Brewster, she was the author of *Tasman* (1907), *Interrogation* (1927), and articles treating Northampton, the drama, etc. She wrote on Cable in *Congregationalist*, CX (December 10, 1925), 816-17.

8. Taplin's letter to Cable, April 20, 1907, is in the Cable Collection at Tulane University.

9. Letter, Adelene Moffat to Mrs. Thomas Shepherd, February 3, 1951, in the archives of the Northampton Historical Society.

10. Wilson, *op. cit.*, p. 213.

Chapter Eleven

1. In general, Negro leaders ceased to think of Cable as a resource. *The Negro Problem* (New York, 1903) contains essays on various aspects of the race problem by Booker T. Washington, W. E. B. DuBois, Charles W. Chesnutt, T. Thomas Fortune, and others. These articles, by men who had once lauded Cable for his support of their cause, commend several white liberals but make no mention of Cable. In another volume of collected essays, *From Servitude to Service* (Boston, 1905), treating educational problems of the Negro in the South, there is no reference to Cable except a comment by William G. Frost, the white president of Berea College, about Cable's praise of the "unique position" of that interracial Kentucky institution. On Cable's association with Washington, see my "George W. Cable and Booker T. Washington," *Journal of Negro Education*, XVII (Fall, 1948), 462-68.

2. Like many another reader of Cable's earlier Creole and quadroon stories, Howells was conditioned to expect Creole characters to have a touch of Negro ancestry. He wrote Cable, October 2, 1918, to praise the book as a return to his best self—"divinely beyond romance; it is poetry"—and to ask whether it was the heroine or her aunts "who had the *tache,* however far, of black ancestry." His mistake, he wrote on October 9, came from reading between the lines of the novel on pages 333-34. Kjell Ekström, "The Cable-Howells Correspondence," *Studia Neophilologica*, XXII (Spring, 1950), 61.

3. Of the attitude of Creoles today toward the Mardi Gras, Sean O'Faolain says, "They take it very lightly, indeed. But let anyone else dare take their words at face value!" "New Orleans," *Holiday*, XXX (November, 1961), 56-57.

4. On the nature and impact of the film, see Everett Carter, "Cultural History Written with Lightning: The Significance of *The Birth of a Nation*," *American Quarterly*, XII (Fall, 1960), 347-57.

5. Helen M. Chesnutt, *Charles Waddell Chesnutt: Pioneer of the Color Line* (Chapel Hill, N. C., 1952), pp. 290-91.

6. "From an Older Time," *Dial*, LXV (November 2, 1918), 346.

7. "Citizen of the Union," *New Republic*, LVII (February 13, 1929), 352.

Selected Bibliography

PRIMARY SOURCES

With the exceptions noted, all of Cable's books were published in New York by Charles Scribner's Sons. For foreign editions and bibliographical descriptions, see Jacob Blanck, comp., *Bibliography of American Literature*, II (New Haven: Yale University Press, 1957), 1-12.

Cable's publications in newspapers, journals, and miscellaneous volumes are too numerous to permit listing here. Most of the important items are cited in footnotes or in the text of this study, and sufficient information is given to make it possible to locate them readily. See also the Index entry on Cable's writings. No complete and fully accurate bibliography of his works is available. The biographical studies by Biklé, Butcher, Ekström, and Turner (1956), listed in Section I of this bibliography, contain useful bibliographies of Cable's miscellaneous publications.

Old Creole Days. 1879.
The Grandissimes. 1880. Revised in 1883.
Madame Delphine. 1881.
The Creoles of Louisiana. 1884.
Dr. Sevier. Boston: J. R. Osgood, 1884. Editions after 1887 published in New York by Charles Scribner's Sons.
The Silent South. 1885. Enlarged edition in 1889.
Bonaventure. 1888.
Strange True Stories of Louisiana. 1889.
The Negro Question. 1890. Enlarged edition, ed. Arlin Turner, Garden City, N. Y.: Doubleday Anchor Books, 1958.
The Busy Man's Bible. Meadville, Pa.: Flood & Vincent, 1891.
A Memory of Roswell Smith. New York: De Vinne Press, 1892.
John March, Southerner. 1894. Issued on February 11, 1895.
Strong Hearts. 1899.
The Cable Story Book. Selections for School Reading, eds. Mary E. Burt and Lucy Leffingwell Cable, 1899.
The Cavalier. 1901.
Bylow Hill. 1902.
Kincaid's Battery. 1908.

Selected Bibliography

"Posson Jone'" and *Père Raphaël.* 1909.
Gideon's Band. 1914.
The Amateur Garden. 1914.
The Flower of the Chapdelaines. 1918.
Lovers of Louisiana. 1918.

SECONDARY SOURCES

I. *Books:*

BIKLÉ, LUCY LEFFINGWELL CABLE. *George W. Cable: His Life and Letters.* New York: Charles Scribner's Sons, 1928. The first book-length study, this biography by one of Cable's daughters tends to stress his associations with his family and with the distinguished men of his time.

BUTCHER, PHILIP. *George W. Cable: The Northampton Years.* New York: Columbia University Press, 1959. Emphasis here is on Cable's significance as a social critic, his relationship with Adelene Moffat, and his connection with the Home Culture Clubs.

CARDWELL, GUY A. *Twins of Genius.* [East Lansing:] Michigan State College Press, 1953. A study of the Mark Twain-Cable relationship, centering on the joint reading tour of 1884-85. It prints many pertinent letters.

DENNIS, MARY CABLE. *The Tail of the Comet.* New York: E. P. Dutton & Co., 1937. The first half of this volume is a memoir, admittedly inattentive to systematic organization and factual details, by one of Cable's daughters.

EKSTRÖM, KJELL. *George Washington Cable: A Study of His Early Life and Work.* Cambridge: Harvard University Press, 1950. Notable for its objectivity, this work gives special attention to the problem of Cable's representation of Creole life and to influences and sources—literary and otherwise—for his early writing.

TURNER, ARLIN. *George W. Cable: A Biography.* Durham, N. C.: Duke University Press, 1956. The only thorough, full-length biography, this is the principal reference work for students of Cable's life.

————. *Mark Twain and George W. Cable.* [East Lansing:] Michigan State University Press, 1960. An account, developed through the presentation of correspondence, of the friendship of Twain and Cable. Letters already in print are omitted, and few of the letters published here are made available in their entirety. Cable's late tributes to Twain are included.

[*179*]

II. *Essays and General References:*

There are so many essays on Cable's life and work that it is not feasible to describe even the more important items here. Many significant essays, including a number published very recently, are cited in footnotes, as are several important general references. There are useful reference bibliographies in the biographical works by Ekström and Turner (1956) mentioned above. The list below, a supplement to the reference bibliography in my book on Cable's Northampton years, is composed of sources used in the preparation of the present study which are *not* cited in the footnotes.

BLISS, ARTHUR AMES. *Theodore Bliss, Publisher and Bookseller: A Study of Character and Life in the Middle Period of the XIX Century.* [Northampton, Mass.:] Northampton Historical Society, 1941. A memoir, first published privately in 1911, which is of interest for its picture of Northampton.

CLEMENS, SAMUEL L. *The Love Letters of Mark Twain.* ed. DIXON WECTER. New York: Harper & Brothers, 1949, pp. 218-40. Twain's colorful comments about Cable, his companion on the reading tour in 1884-85, must not be taken literally; but neither must they be discounted.

COWIE, ALEXANDER. *The Rise of the American Novel.* New York: American Book Company, 1948, pp. 556-67. Useful for plot summaries and critical appraisals, generally sound, of Cable's novels. Minor factual errors have been corrected by Cable's later biographers.

FATOUT, PAUL. *Mark Twain on the Lecture Circuit.* Bloomington: Indiana University Press, 1960, pp. 204-31. A thorough study of the Twain-Cable reading tour of 1884-85, based on a variety of sources.

JOHNSON, CLIFTON. *Historic Hampshire in the Connecticut Valley.* Springfield, Mass.: Milton Bradley Co., 1932. An able history of the Massachusetts county in which Cable spent half of his life. The emphasis is on physical features, personalities, and social movements.

LARKIN, OLIVER W. *Art and Life in America.* New York: Rinehart & Co., 1949. Because Cable was acquainted with artists and deeply interested in art, this history of the arts in America and their social background is very useful.

LOGAN, RAYFORD W. *The Negro in American Life and Thought; The Nadir: 1877-1901.* New York: Dial Press, 1954, pp. 239-74. A fine study of a neglected aspect of American history, this volume includes an analysis of the picture of Negro life presented in books and popular literature of the time.

Selected Bibliography

MOTT, FRANK LUTHER. *A History of American Magazines: 1885-1905.* Cambridge: The Belknap Press of Harvard University Press, 1957. The standard work on the subject, this is useful in considering Cable's problems as a contributor to assorted journals of his day.

PORTER, DOROTHY B. "David Ruggles, 1810-1849; Hydropathic Practitioner," *Journal of the National Medical Association,* XLIX (January and March, 1957), 67-72; 130-34. The most complete study of the Northampton Water Cure establishment.

RUBIN, LOUIS D., JR., and John Rees Moore, eds. *The Idea of an American Novel.* New York: Thomas Y. Crowell Co., 1961. A collection of short documents on the American novel by outstanding critics and novelists.

SHEFFIELD, CHARLES A., ed. *The History of Florence, Massachusetts.* Florence, Mass., 1895. Here in detail is the story of the Northampton Association of Education and Industry and of other movements and persons whose influence was reflected in Cable's life. Published by the editor.

TALLANT, ROBERT, ed. *New Orleans City Guide.* (American Guide Series.) Boston: Houghton Mifflin Co., 1952. This revision of the guide first prepared by the WPA is a comprehensive portrait of the city that was Cable's principal subject. There are many references to him and to scenes and characters described in his books.

————. *The Romantic New Orleanians.* New York: E. P. Dutton & Co., 1950. A fine social history of Cable's native city.

TURNER, ARLIN, ed. *Southern Stories.* New York: Rinehart & Co., 1960, pp. xi-xl. For this collection the editor has supplied an introduction, a bibliographical note, and a "Southern Chronology."

TYLER, HENRY M. *The Beginnings of the Northampton Social and Literary Club.* Northampton, Mass.: Published by The Club, 1925, 17 pp. The most complete published account of the history of an organization to which Cable belonged for many years. Details of his activity as a member may be found in the bound volumes of minutes on deposit at Forbes Library in Northampton.

WILSON, EDMUND. *Patriotic Gore: Studies in the Literature of the American Civil War.* New York: Oxford University Press, 1962. A compilation of provocative essays, most of them first published in *New Yorker.* Despite certain inaccuracies, Chapter XIII is particularly useful.

WOODWARD, C. VANN. *The Strange Career of Jim Crow.* Rev. ed. New York: Oxford University Press, 1957. A study of the Negro's loss of civil rights during the years Cable was championing his cause.

Index

Names of characters in Cable's novels and other fiction are followed by the title—in parenthesis—of the work in which they appear.

Index

De Charleau, Colonel ("Belles Dem-
oiselles Plantation"), 37-38
De Forest, John W., 166
Délicieuse, Madame ("Madame
Délicieuse"), 40
Delphine (Madame Delphine Car-
raze) (Madame Delphine), 57-58,
166
D'Hemecourt, Pauline ("Café des
Exilés"), 40
Dial, 158
Dixon, Thomas, 162
Dodge, Mary Mapes, 67
Double Dealer, 166
Douglass, Frederick, 87
Doyle, A. Conan, 133, 139
Dred, 52
Dreiser, Theodore, 162
"Drop Shot," Cable's Picayune col-
umn, 23
DuBois, W. E. B., 151
Ducour, Camille ("Attalie Brouil-
lard"), 101-2
Dunbar, Paul Laurence, 129
Durel, M. (Lovers of Louisiana),
159
Durel, Rosalie (Lovers of Louisi-
ana), 159

Edwards Congregational Church
(Northampton), 88, 154
Edwards, Jonathan, 87
Eliot, T. S., 165
Emerson, Ralph Waldo, 87

Falkner, Colonel William, 165-66
"Fall of the House of Usher, The,"
38
Famous Adventures and Prison Es-
capes of the Civil War, 100
Faulkner, William, 166
Ferber, Edna, 152
Ferry, Ned (The Cavalier), 141-42,
150
Field, Eugene, 115, 128-29
Fisk University, 107
Florence, Massachusetts, 87, 107

Fontenette ("The Entomologist"),
138, 150
Fontenette, Mrs. ("The Entomolo-
gist"), 138-39
Fool's Errand, A, 84
Forrest, Nathan Bedford, 23
Fortune (The Flower of the Chap-
delaines), 155
Fox, John, Jr., 162
Frederic, Harold, 117, 126
Free men and women of color
("f.m.c." and "f.w.c."), gens de
couleur libres, 20-21, 50-51, 57
Frowenfeld, Joseph (The Grandis-
simes), 47-50, 52, 55-56, 64, 70,
83, 90, 117, 125, 161
Fuller, Henry Blake, 126

Garland, Hamlin, 126-27, 129
Garnet, Barbara (John March,
Southerner), 117, 120, 123
Garnet, Major (John March, South-
erner), 117-18, 120
Garrison, William Lloyd, 83, 87
Garroters, The, 115
George, 'Sieur ("'Sieur George"),
33-36
Gholson, Scott (The Cavalier), 142
Gilder, Richard Watson, 27-28, 60,
62, 67-68, 73, 75, 109, 115-16,
126, 128, 134, 138, 150
Gilmore, Mr. and Mrs. (Gideon's
Band), 153-54
Glasgow, Ellen, 162
Gone With the Wind, 166
Good Housekeeping, 103
Grady, Henry W., 84, 116
Grandissime, Honoré (The Grandis-
simes), 47, 50-51, 54-55
Grandissime, Honoré, free man of
color (The Grandissimes), 50, 83
Gregory ("The Solitary"), 136-37

Hale, Edward Everett, 75
Halliday, Fannie (John March,
Southerner), 118
Halliday, General (John March,
Southerner), 118
Hammond, John C., 148

[185]

Index